HANDBOOK ON INFLAMMATORY BOWEL DISEASE

(VOLUME 1)

(Peer Reviewed Book)

Handbook on Inflammatory Bowel Disease (Volume 1)

(Peer Reviewed Book)

Dr. Khushboo Gupta, Assistant Professor, Trilok Singh TT College, Lakshmangarh, Sikar, Rajasthan, India

Dr. Gopeswar Mukharjee, M.B.B.S., D.C.P & amp; M.D. (Path), Ph.D. (Path) Professor & amp; Dean, Brainware University, Kolkata, West Bengal, India

Dr. Esaivani KB, Senior Resident, Dept. of Pathology, Arunai Medical College and Hospital, Tiruvannamalai, Tamilnadu, India

Dr. Sangeeta, Assistant Professor, Home- Science (Food & Nutrition), Ramabai Govt. Women Post Graduate College- Akbarpur, Ambedkar Nagar- Uttar-Pradesh, India

Dr. K Anuradha, lecturer, SRR & CVR Govt. Degree College, Machavaram, Vijayawada, Andhra Pradesh, India.

Dr. Poonam Jethwani, Assistant Professor, School of Allied Health Scienecs, Jaipur National University, Jaipur, India

HEMAKSHEE PUBLICATION

Handbook on Inflammatory Bowel Disease
(Volume 1)

Edition: 2024
ISBN: 978-81-969920-0-2

Published by Hemakshee Publication
Printed and Distributed by pothi.com

HEMAKSHEE PUBLICATION
Sikar, Rajasthan, India

Email: hemaksheepublication@gmail.com

Contents

S.No.	Chapter	Page No.
1.	Etiology, Differential Diagnosis, Prevention, and Treatment of Inflammatory Bowel Disease (IBD) **Dr. Praveen Katiyar, Shivam Agarwal, Anurag Mishra**	1
2.	Prevention of Inflammatory Bowel Disease (IBD) **Dr. Prof. Gopeswar Mukherjee**	21
3.	Quality of Life of Inflammatory Bowel Disease Patients **Baijnath Das, Shivam Agarwal, Dr. (Prof.) Navneet Kumar**	29
4.	Malnutrition and Inflammatory Disease **Dr. Praveen Katiyar, Chandan Kumar**	52
5.	The Role of Diet in Inflammatory Bowel Diseases **Jige Sandipan Babasaheb**	87

Foreword

I often have discussion with my students taking the course in Nutrition and Critical Care on the hiatus that exists between the theory and practice of therapeutic nutrition and the ways of bridging it. Studying each disorder or syndrome as a  single chapter of a book was sometimes a constraint. I am glad that a solution has been sought in the form of this handbook dealing with all pertinent aspects of a specific disorder, which can be of benefit to medical, paramedical and nutrition fraternity. It gives me immense pleasure to write the foreword for this much needed compendium.

Inflammatory Bowel Disease (IBD) is complex and multifactorial. Environmental factors and genetic factors interact, leading to a dysfunctional relationship between intestinal microbiome and immune system due to abnormal intestinal barrier function. It encompasses both ulcerative colitis and Crohn's disease. IBD has become a significant global health concern affecting >0.3% of the world population. While the disease prevalence in India may be lower compared to western countries, the country's vast population translates into a large number of individuals affected with IBD. With the significant disease burden of IBD in India, we need to gear up to face the challenges of managing large number of patients. This can take the shape of dual pronged strategy: tackling the explosion of the disease and taking definitive steps to prevent the disease. IBD significantly affects the life of the patients and their families, as lifelong modification of behavior, lifestyle and eating habits is required. The lack of clear information of nutrition and diet in IBD pushes patients to seek information from other sources and ultimately increase the risk of self-imposed dietary restrictions with important negative consequences on patients' health.

The content about IBD, in this handbook remains current. The chapters in this book have tried to answer questions related to what, why, how much, which route and have also emphasized the need to individualize the treatment as well as nutrition. IBD is a complex area of therapeutics and it is important to remain updated with the latest knowledge and expert opinion in the field. This handbook is, therefore, highly relevant and topical. It will help guide the therapies well. The editors have been successful in compiling a single volume focused on IBD with fitting reference to physiological background. As a valuable resource for practitioners caring for IBD patients, it contains chapters written by experts who provide theoretical and practical information on important areas of IBD including nutrition and diet. Educators will find this text effective in promoting learning among students who intend to become tomorrow's practitioners.

Each chapter of the handbook succinctly presents relevant content that is interesting and easy to understand. I commend the efforts of the authors and the editors for drawing together this impressive volume.

Monika Jain, M.Sc. (Nutrition), PhD
Professor (Food Science and Nutrition) Banasthali
Vidyapith (Deemed to be University)
Rajasthan, India

Preface

This book titled **"Handbook on Inflammatory Bowel Disease (Volume 1)"** is primarily intended to be a collection of peer reviewed and plagiarism free chapters written by research scholars, academicians, scientists, doctors and faculty members of their respective fields. Chapters of this book particularly based on topics such as etiology differential diagnosis, prevention and treatment of inflammatory bowel disease (IBD); malnutrition and IBD, role of yoga & meditation in IBD, yoga techniques & quality of life in patients with IBD, role of diet in IBD, use of micro-organisms in prevention & treatment of IBD, role of remission diet in IBD and pediatric IBD compass.

It seems to be the first-ever Indian published document fully focused on **Inflammatory Bowel Disease** and aims to orient the readers about the multidimensional association and impact of inflammatory bowel disease on physiology, psychology and quality of life of an individual.

We envisage this book to serve as a professional reference for researchers and practitioners in their relevant scientific field. This book will be very useful for students all over in India and Abroad, academicians, medical doctors, dietitians, nutritionists, health care workers, public health specialists, community science specialists, community development professionals, programmers of national and international agencies as well as libraries of relevant collages and institutions.

This book should be of interest to policy makers, bureaucrats, economists and community scientists and can be a reference material for development industry.

This is the sixteenth book in the series of community upliftment. You can see the details of previous books in the section of list of publications at the end of the book.

We are extremely thankful to **Monika Jain ma'am**, M.Sc. (Nutrition), PhD Professor (Food Science and Nutrition) Banasthali Vidyapith (Deemed to be University), Rajasthan, India for her best wishes and direction. She is the mentor, role model and wonderful light house of Dr. Khushboo Gupta (chief editor of this book). As a beneficiary of Monika Jain madam's, extreme intelligence and sharp insight no words of Dr. Khushboo can express and encompass her sincere and deep feelings of gratitude and thankfulness that she have for her ma'am.

With great pleasure, we would like to extend our sincere thanks to all the authors of the chapters for reporting their thoughts and experience related to their research and also for patiently addressing reviewer's comments and diligently adhering hectic deadlines to have the book published in timely manner. Their constant support and cooperation has made our task as editors a pleasure. We believe that this book is an important contribution to the community in addressing research work from numerous domains of Health.

It is our sincere hope that many more will join us in this time-critical endeavour and this book will stimulate discussions and generate helpful comments to improve future projects.

Happy reading and feedback awaited.

Dr. Khushboo Gupta
Dr. Gopeswar Mukharjee
Dr. Esai Vani
Dr. Sangeeta
Dr. K Anuradha
Dr. Poonam Jethwani

Introduction

Dr. Khushboo Gupta

Assistant Professor

Trilok Singh TT College

Lakshmangarh, Sikar (Rajasthan)

Email: drkhushboogupta2017@gmail.com

An aberrant immune response to gut microbiota results in recurrent episodes of gastrointestinal tract inflammation, which are the hallmark of a group of chronic illnesses known as inflammatory bowel disease (IBD). The two forms of idiopathic intestinal disease that make up inflammatory bowel disease are distinguished from one another by the location and extent of their involvement in the bowel wall. (i) The mucosa of the colon is diffusely inflamed in ulcerative colitis. Proctitis, or ulcerative colitis that primarily affects the rectum, can also spread to the sigmoid (proctosigmoiditis), beyond the sigmoid (distal ulcerative colitis), or affect the entire colon, including the cecum (pancolitis). (ii) Transmural ulceration of any part of the gastrointestinal system, most frequently affecting the colon and terminal ileum, is a consequence of Crohn's disease. Both conditions are categorised according to their location and degree (mild, moderate, or severe). The three phenotypes of Crohn's disease are penetrating, stricturing, and inflammatory.

Both Crohn's disease and ulcerative colitis include a wide range of extraintestinal symptoms in addition to the GI tract. While the illnesses can be differentiated from one another in the majority of patients. It is impossible to classify IBD because about 10% of patients have identical traits.

There is a hereditary tendency to both conditions; they are both extremely morbid, and none is treatable. Lastly, there is a higher chance of colorectal cancer with both.

Prevalence

Prevalence of IBD increases day by day due to changing lifestyle, dietary habits and environmental factors. Individuals of all age groups are suffering from IBD in India and worldwide but occurrence of IBD in old age is lower as compared to younger age groups. Geographical variances are seen as southern and urban regions of India may have a relatively higher prevalence compared to northern and rural areas. IBD is considered a global disease and its prevalence has been increasing over the past few decades.

Symptoms (World Gastroenterology Organization)

- Diarrhoea can be linked to mucus or blood; it can also happen at night, and faecal incontinence is a regular occurrence.
- When ulcerative colitis is limited to the rectum, some patients may exhibit constipation.
- Severe urgency, tenesmus, and abdominal discomfort are other typical complaints.

- Pain in the right lower quadrant can be a symptom of Crohn's disease, while pain in the left lower quadrant can be a sign of ulcerative colitis.
- With Crohn's disease, nausea and vomiting are more frequent
- Pallor may be observed, depending on the anaemia;
- Common symptoms include tachycardia, anxiety, fever, and dehydration.
- Severe discomfort, fever, stomach distension, chills, and lethargic behaviour are possible symptoms of toxic megacolon. Because it can be fatal if ignored, this surgical emergency should always be taken into consideration.

- Rectal prolapse, anal fistulas, and abscesses are all possible signs of Crohn's disease.

- On a digital rectal exam, occult blood is frequently seen.

- One may only observe growth regression in children.

Diagnosis

Inflammatory Bowel Disease (IBD) poses a diagnostic challenge due to its complex and heterogeneous nature. Clinical evaluation involves a combination of patient history, physical examination, and laboratory tests. Common symptoms include abdominal pain, diarrhea, weight loss, and fatigue. Diagnostic tools such as endoscopy, colonoscopy, and imaging studies like MRI or CT scans help visualize the extent and severity of inflammation. Biopsies aid in confirming the diagnosis

Management

IBD management includes medical management (anti-inflammatory medications, immunomodulators, biologics and JK inhibitors), nutritional therapy (enteral nutrition and dietary modification), surgical interventions (resections, ileostomy and colostomy).

Recent Trends in Inflammatory Bowel Disease (IBD) Management and Treatment

1. Targeted therapies and precision medicine

- **Biosimilars:** Increased availability of biosimilar medications offers cost-effective alternatives to biologics without compromising efficacy.

- **Personalized treatment plans:** Growing emphasis on genetic profiling and biomarker-guided therapy tailors treatment strategies to individual patient characteristics.

2. Advanced biologics and small molecule inhibitors

- **Next-generation biologics:** Novel biologics with different mechanisms of action, such as anti-IL-23 and anti-IL-12 agents, expand the treatment arsenal.

- **JAK inhibitors:** Small molecule Janus kinase inhibitors like upadacitinib and filgotinib provide additional options, particularly for patients intolerant to or failing biologics.

3. Top-down treatment approach

- **Early intervention:** Shifting towards a "top-down" approach involves initiating more potent therapies earlier in the disease course to achieve faster and sustained remission.

4. Telemedicine and digital health

- **Remote monitoring:** Telemedicine facilitates regular check-ins, allowing healthcare providers to monitor patient progress and adjust treatment plans without in-person visits.

- **Mobile applications:** Apps for symptom tracking, medication adherence, and dietary management enhance patient engagement and self-management.

5. Microbiome-targeted therapies

- **Fecal microbiota transplantation (FMT):** Ongoing research explores FMT's potential in restoring a balanced gut microbiome, influencing disease activity in IBD.

- **Prebiotics and probiotics:** Proactive use of prebiotics and specific probiotic strains aims to modulate the gut microbiota and improve symptoms.

6. Patient-centric care

- **Shared decision making:** Encouraging active involvement of patients in treatment decisions fosters a collaborative and personalized approach.

- **Patient education:** Increased emphasis on educating patients about their condition, treatment options, and lifestyle modifications enhances overall disease management.

7. Surgical innovations

- **Minimally invasive surgery:** Advancements in laparoscopic and robotic techniques reduce postoperative complications and recovery times.

- **Strictureplasty:** For Crohn's disease, innovative surgical approaches like strictureplasty aim to preserve bowel length and function.

8. Nutritional approaches

- **Exclusive enteral nutrition (EEN) optimization:** Fine-tuning EEN protocols and exploring its combination with other dietary interventions for improved efficacy.

- **Enteral nutrition in crohn's disease:** Ongoing research on the role of enteral nutrition in inducing and maintaining remission, especially in pediatric cases.

9. Real-world evidence and comparative effectiveness research

- **Long-term outcomes:** A growing focus on real-world evidence helps evaluate the long-term effectiveness and safety of various treatment strategies beyond clinical trials.

- **Comparative studies:** Comparative effectiveness research guides clinicians in choosing the most appropriate therapy based on real-world outcomes.

Prognosis

The severity of the illness and the responsiveness to treatment determine the prognosis for both UC and CD. The stool markers calprotectin and lactoferrin can be used to identify CD recurrence following surgery. There is evidence to suggest that they can be utilised to forecast flares in the future. However, compared to the general population, people with IBD typically have substantially higher mortality rates. Primary diseases, infections, and respiratory ailments are among the causes of death. Heart illness does not increase the chance of dying from IBD. Lastly, IBD patients have very high psychological morbidity and low quality of life.

For long-term UC patients, screening for dysplasia must continue. For people who have had colorectal cancer for 30 years or longer, the cumulative risk is thought to be as high as 30%. Liver failure is the result of primary sclerosing cholangitis' extraintestinal manifestation.

Impact of IBD on Different body organs

Inflammatory Bowel Disease (IBD), comprising Crohn's disease and ulcerative colitis, primarily affects the gastrointestinal tract (hemorrhage, strictures, colon perforation, anal fistulas, pelvic or perirectal abscesses, toxic megacolon, cholangiocarcinoma, colon cancer).

However, its impact can extend beyond the intestines (extra intestinal, i.e., osteoporosis, deep vein thrombosis, anemia, gallstones, primary sclerosing cholangitis, aphthous ulcers, arthritis, iritis, pyoderma gangrenosum), affecting various organs and systems in the body

1. Gastrointestinal tract

- **Crohn's disease:** Can affect any part of the digestive tract, from the mouth to the anus, leading to inflammation, ulcers, and strictures.

- **Ulcerative colitis:** Primarily involves the colon and rectum, causing inflammation and ulceration of the colonic lining.

2. Joints and musculoskeletal system

- IBD patients may experience arthritis, joint pain, and inflammation, known as enteropathic arthritis.

- Conditions like ankylosing spondylitis and sacroiliitis can occur, impacting the spine and pelvic joints.

3. Skin

- Dermatological manifestations are common, including erythema nodosum and pyodermagangrenosum, characterized by painful skin lesions.

4. Eyes

- Uveitis, inflammation of the middle layer of the eye, is a potential complication in IBD.

- Dry eyes and other eye conditions may also occur.

5. Liver

- Primary sclerosing cholangitis (PSC) is associated with IBD, causing inflammation and scarring of the bile ducts in the liver.

- Hepatic steatosis (fatty liver) and autoimmune hepatitis can also be observed.

6. Kidneys

- IBD-related kidney complications include nephrolithiasis (kidney stones) and amyloidosis.

- Glomerulonephritis, affecting the filtering units of the kidneys, is a rare but serious complication.

7. Cardiovascular System

- IBD patients may have an increased risk of cardiovascular diseases, possibly linked to chronic inflammation.

- Vasculitis, inflammation of blood vessels, can occur in some cases.

8. Lungs

- Pulmonary complications include inflammation, pneumonia, and bronchiectasis.

- Conditions like interstitial lung disease may be associated with IBD.

9. Blood

- Anemia is a common complication due to chronic inflammation, nutritional deficiencies, or blood loss.

- Thromboembolic events may occur, increasing the risk of blood clots.

10. Central nervous system

- Neurological complications are rare but can include peripheral neuropathy, seizures, and cerebrovascular events.

11. Psychological impact

- IBD is associated with an increased risk of mental health issues, including anxiety and depression, affecting the overall well-being of individuals.

Conclusions

In the past two decades, advancements in understanding IBD's underlying mechanisms have transformed diagnosis and treatment paradigms. A personalized approach, integrating medical, surgical, and psychosocial strategies, has become pivotal in optimizing patient outcomes. It's crucial for individuals with IBD to receive comprehensive care involving gastroenterologists and specialists in related fields to manage and address potential complications in different organs.

Ongoing research and the advent of innovative therapies hold promise for further enhancing the management of IBD. Regular monitoring and a multidisciplinary approach can contribute to better outcomes and improved quality of life for those living with IBD.

Biography
(Dr. Khushboo Gupta)

Dr. Khushboo Gupta is a PhD Home Science (Food Science and Nutrition) from Banasthali Vidyapith, Newai, India. She has been teaching subject including food chemistry, food analysis, therapeutic nutrition, human nutrition, human physiology and community nutrition, etc. 
Presently she is working as Assistant Professor in Trilok Singh TT College, Laxmangarh, Sikar, Rajasthan.

She is MSc Gold medalist and had **cleared UGC-NET and RPSC-SET examination.** Dr Gupta holds Advance Diploma in French Language from Banasthali Vidyapith; Diploma in Naturopathy and Yoga (NDDY) from Gandhi Smarak Prakritik Chikitsa Samiti (Regd.), New Delhi; Certificate in Homeopathic Medicinal System conducted by Vardhman Mahaveer Open University, Kota and Certificate in Statistical Techniques and Applications. She has featured in several programs of All India Radio and Radio Banasthali (FM 90.4).

Dr. Khushboo is actively involved in community activities especially those concerned with self-employment, health and wellness, optimum nutrition and how to improve quality of life of a person and family. She is the keynote speaker and founder of her YouTube channel "Dietitian Ki Salah" through which she provides education related to optimum health, wellness and nutrition to masses. Dr. Gupta has published about more than 30 research papers in reputed national and international journals; 7 book chapters in different edited books, several news paper and magazine articles related to health, nutrition and new food product formulation. She authored one book related to elderly nutrition; edited fourteen books related to community science, food science and nutrition, health and wellness, issues with girls, health for all, sustainable development, food safety and security and millets for upliftment of the individuals of the society. She presented her research work in more than 26 national and international conferences. Her research is primarily in the area of food processing entrepreneurial skill Inculcation and geriatric nutrition. **The patent office, Government of India has granted a patent to Dr. Khushboo for her research on food formulation using RSM.** Dr. Gupta has successfully completed more than 30 courses on various diverse topics organized by SWAYAM, UNICEF, WHO and Cornell University.

In past she had worked as Assistant Professor (Food and Nutrition) in Modi University, Laxmangarh, Sikar; worked as Master Trainer in Agriculture University, Kota. During her PhD she had worked as UGC- SRF in Banasthali Vidyapith, Newai. One feather in her cap is that she had worked as regular trainee dietitian in dietetics department of Post Graduate Institute of Medical Education and Research (PGIMER), Chandigarh and got her short-term attachment certificate. She won many awards in different seminars and conferences for her contribution in scientific world. Apart from them, she is rewarded with **Teacher Honour award** by Lions Club Kota South (September, 2017); '**Award of Honour**' given by All Rajasthan Qualified Homoeopathic Doctors Association in Homoeopathic Scientific Seminar,

2017 and **Excellence Academician Award** given by Akhil Bhartiya Agrawal Mahasabha (Reg), kota Branch (2023).

She is the life member of many reputed institutes i.e. Nutrition Society of India, Indian Dietetic Association, The Indian Science Congress Association and Institute of Scholars and giving her services for upliftment of community.

Biography
(Dr. Gopeswar Mukharjee)

Gopeswar Mukharjee M.B.B.S., D.C.P., M.D. (Path.), Ph. D. (Path). Dsc (hon) is presently working as the Professor & dean of Brainware University, Kolkata.

He has an experience of working for more than 20 years as pathologist in WBHS & more than 12 yrs as M.O including MOIC in Blood Bank. He is trained on HLA Techniques from AIIMS, New Delhi & Molecular Genetics pathology from Kolkata, W.B and trained on Laboratory Diagnosis of Hemophilia conducted by Hemophilia Federation (India). Past working status of him are as follows: (i) Hony consultant pathologist of NH-Multi Speciality Hospital, Barasat; (ii) Hony consultant pathologist of Barasat Cancer Hospital; (iii) Ex-Pathologist and Guest Lecturer, Department of Pathology, Institute of Post Graduate Ay. Education & Research at SVSP, Kolkata, Govt. of West Bengal; (iv) Co-Supervisor of Ay. Post Graduate Students (M.D.) of the University of Calcutta and West Bengal University of health sciences, (v) Co-Supervisor of Ph. D. programme.

He wrote books and multiple papers in national and international scientific journals and presented his work in various conferences and seminars

Biography
Dr Esaivani KB

Dr Esaivani KB was born in Tamilnadu. Being raised by proud parents, she is a more passionate and a budding pathologist. She started writing and publishing journals since 2022. This is her first book as editor in which she was very much interested to do.

She completed her undergraduation in Government erode medical College. She is also a proud alumini of prestigious Mysore medical College where she completed her MD pathology successfully. She quotes "Keep yourself surrounded by people who encourage you" that keeps her always pushing to accept the failures and reach lifetime goals. Presently she is working as **Senior Resident, Dept. of Pathology,** Arunai Medical College and Hospital, Tiruvannamalai, India.

Biography
(Dr. Sangeeta)

Dr. Sangeeta is working as Assistant Professor in Home-Science (Food & Nutrition) at Ramabai Govt. Women Post Graduate College- Akbarpur, Ambedkarnagar- Uttar-Pradesh. She has 13 year experience of teaching to  graduates and Post graduate students. She Qualifies the U. G. C. NET Examination in June 2005. Her more than 35 research papers have been published in National and International Journals and Proceedings of seminars as well as 12 Book chapters published from National and International Publishers. She has more than 10 societies and institutional life Membership

She got many prestigious awards such as Best Teacher Award, Young Scientist Award; Award from Higher Education, Excellence Academician Award, Best Oral Presentation Award etc. she had organized 6 webinars and 07 International Conferences. She was the member of organizing committees of 2 national conferences. She wrote 2 books and edited 6 books. She is the member and coordinator of various college committees including IQAC. Dr. Sangeeta presented her papers in about 23 International conferences and 25 national conferences.

Biography
Dr. K Anuradha

Dr K Anuradha has done her postgraduation and Ph.D. in Food Science and Nutrition from Sri Padmavathi Mahila Visvavidyalayam, Tirupati, Andhra Pradesh, India. Presently she is working as lecturer, SRR & CVR Govt. Degree College, Machavaram, Vijayawada, Andhra Pradesh, India. 

She has cleared diploma in "Quality Assurance and ISO 9000" from the Indian Institute of Management and Technology, Chennai and a certificate course on "Gut Check: Exploring Your Microbiome" from the University of Colorado Boulder.

Dr K Anuradha worked as dietician for more than ten years in various reputed teaching hospitals. She has been teaching Food Science and Technology for the past six years. In this short tenure she published more than eight research papers in reputed national and international journals, two book chapters in two different books and she is currently working on food waste minimisation.

She has been featured in several programs on All India Radio and is a life member of many reputed institutes like the Indian Public Health Association, Kolkata.

Biography
Dr. Poonam Jethwani

Dr. Poonam Jethwani has received her undergraduate and post graduate degree from G.B. Pant university of Agriculture and Technology, Pantnagar, India in 2013 and 2015 respectively. She was awarded Ph.D. Degree in the field of food and nutrition in 2018 by Punjab Agricultural University, Ludhiana, India. She got first rank in ICAR-NET SRF examination and has also qualified UGC NET JRF in 2015. She has a total experience of 6+ years in teaching and research. Currently she is working as Assistant Professor in School of Allied Health Sciences, Jaipur National University, Jaipur. She has an expertise in the field of food science, food product development and nutritional analysis, Food adulteration, food safety and Community Nutrition. She has more than 10 publications in reputed journals and books in her field of expertise. She is an active life member of esteemed Nutrition Society of India, Indian Dietetics Association and Association of Food Scientists and Technologists, India. She has actively participated in various conference, workshop, seminars, PDPs and FDPs and also been a part of organizing committee member of international conference. She has been awarded Young Scientist Award by All India Institute of Medical Science, Delhi in 2012 for the best poster presentation.

List of Contributors

- **Anurag Mishra**, Ph.D. Scholar, Department of M.L.T School of Health Sciences, CSJM University Kanpur.
- **Arushi Jain**, Research scholar, Lady Irwin College, University of Delhi
- **Baijnath Das** Assistant Professor, Teerthanker Mahaveer University College of Paramedical Sciences, Moradabad.
- **Chandan Kumar**, Ph.D. Scholar, School of Health Sciences, CSJM University Kanpur.
- **Dr. (Prof.) Navneet Kumar**, Vice Principal, Teerthanker Mahaveer University College of Paramedical Sciences, Moradabad.
- **Dr. Kavana G Venkatappa**, MBBS. MD. Professor & Head, Department of Physiology, Haveri Institute of Medical Sciences, Haveri, Karnataka, India
- **Dr. Praveen Katiyar**, Assistant Professor, School of Health Sciences, CSJM University Kanpur.
- **Dr. Prof. Gopeswar Mukherjee**, M.B.B.S., D.C.P & M.D(Path), Ph.D. (Path) Professor & Dean, Brainware University, Kolkata
- **Dr. Rosy Kumari**, Assistant Professor, Department of Home Science, Patna Women's College, Patna University (Autonomous), Bihar, India
- **Dr. Sparsha Deep EM**, MBBS. MD. Professor & Head, Department of Pharmacology, Shridevi

Institute of Medical Sciences & Research Hospital, Tumakuru, Karnataka, India

- **Jige Sandipan Babasaheb,** Assistant Professor and Head Department of Botany, Sant Ramdas College Ghansawangi, Dist- Jalna Maharashtra
- **Ms. Geethanjali R,** 200hr RY certified (Rishikesh), CCYPI from MDNIY (Delhi), YCB Level 1 Certified, MA Yoga., (Uttarkand Open University); Yoga Trainer at CCR, Maldives.
- **Shivam Agarwal,** Assistant Professor, Teerthanker Mahaveer University College of Paramedical Sciences, Moradabad.

If readers have any query related to any chapter of the book, kindly contact with the corresponding author of the chapter. Authors of the chapters are responsible for their work.

1.

Etiology, Differential Diagnosis, Prevention, and Treatment of Inflammatory Bowel Disease (IBD)

Dr. Praveen Katiyar[1*], Shivam Agarwal[2], Anurag Mishra[3]

[1*]Assistant Professor, School of Health Sciences,

CSJM University Kanpur.

Email: drpraveenkatiyar@gmail.com

[2]Assistant Professor, Teerthanker Mahaveer University

College of Paramedical Sciences, Moradabad.

Email: shivamagarwal50283@gmail.com

[3]Ph.D. Scholar, Department of M.L.T School of Health Sciences,

CSJM University Kanpur.

Email: Mishra.anurag1989@gmail.com

Abstract

Crohn's disease (CD) and ulcerative colitis (UC) are the two primary subtypes of the complex gastrointestinal illness known as inflammatory bowel disease (IBD).

The prevalence of IBD is increasing globally, primarily in developed regions, with genetic predisposition, immune dysregulation, environmental factors, microbiota dysbiosis, and epigenetic modifications contributing to its etiology. The pathogenesis involves immune dysregulation, T-cell activation, cytokine production, barrier dysfunction, microbiota dysbiosis, and epithelial cell damage. IBD presents with general and specific symptoms, and diagnosis relies on a comprehensive approach, including clinical assessment, laboratory tests, endoscopy, imaging, genetic testing, histopathological analysis, and multidisciplinary evaluation.

Keywords: IBD, Crohn's disease, Ulcerative Colitis, Prevalence, Etiology, Pathogenesis, Diagnosis.

1. IBD: A chronic gastrointestinal disorder

Chronic inflammation of the digestive tract is the hallmark of Inflammatory Bowel Disease (IBD), a chronic and complex gastrointestinal disorder. It includes two primary subtypes: Ulcerative Colitis (UC) and Crohn's disease (CD), which differ significantly in their anatomical and histological involvement of the gastrointestinal tract but have comparable symptoms and diagnostic difficulties.

2. A heterogeneous spectrum of disease

Ulcerative colitis and Crohn's disease are two different IBD phenotypes that differ in their histological, endoscopic, and clinical characteristics:

2.1. Crohn's disease (CD)

- Typically affects any part of the digestive tract, from the mouth to the anus.

- Features transmural inflammation, "skip lesions," and complications such as fistulas and strictures.

- Extraintestinal manifestations, diarrhea, weight loss, and stomach pain are typical symptoms.

2.2. Ulcerative colitis (UC)

- Confined to the colon and rectum, affecting the mucosal layer.

- Predominant symptoms include bloody diarrhea and rectal bleeding.

- Complications include toxic megacolon and an increased risk of colorectal cancer.

3. Prevalence

IBD has become a major global public health concern due to its significant increase in incidence and prevalence in recent years. The disease primarily affects people in developed nations, with North America and Europe having the highest prevalence. Based on epidemiological data, the estimated number of individuals with inflammatory bowel disease (IBD) in the United States and Europe is over 3 million. As of 2021, 1.6 million Americans were diagnosed with Crohn's disease, and 907,000 with Ulcerative Colitis.

4. Etiology

4.1. Genetic predisposition

- **Polygenic nature**: IBD is a complex, polygenic disorder, involving multiple genes. Certain genetic variations increase susceptibility, and a family history of IBD significantly elevates the risk.
- **Key genes:** Variations in genes like NOD2, IL23R, and ATG16L1 are associated with higher IBD risk. These genes are involved in immune regulation and gut barrier function.

4.2. Dysregulated immune response

- **Immune system aberrations:** In IBD, the body's own gut tissue is unintentionally attacked by the immune system. In the gastrointestinal tract, chronic inflammation is caused by abnormalities in immune cells, specifically T lymphocytes.
- **Loss of tolerance:** Normally, the immune system tolerates beneficial gut bacteria. In IBD, this tolerance breaks down, leading to an excessive immune response against harmless gut microbes.

4.3. Environmental factors

- **Dietary factors:** Certain diets, especially those high in processed foods, sugars, and unhealthy fats, are linked to increased IBD risk. Conversely, diets rich in fruits, vegetables, and fiber appear to have a protective effect.
- **Smoking:** Cigarette smoking, notably, is a significant risk factor for Crohn's disease. It

worsens the disease's severity and reduces response to treatment.

- **Infections:** Infections of the gastrointestinal tract, especially in children, may set off an aberrant immune response, which raises the risk of developing IBD.

4.4. Microbiota dysbiosis

- **Altered gut microbiota:** IBD patients often have imbalances in their gut microbiota. Reduction in beneficial bacteria and overgrowth of harmful bacteria can contribute to chronic inflammation.
- **Role of antibiotics:** Early exposure to antibiotics, which disrupt the gut microbiota, might contribute to the development of IBD, especially in genetically predisposed individuals.

4.5. Epigenetic modifications

- **DNA Methylation:** Gene expression can be impacted by epigenetic modifications like DNA methylation without changing the underlying DNA sequence. Patients with IBD have been found to have abnormal methylation patterns, which affect inflammation and immune responses.

4.6. Intestinal barrier dysfunction

- **Mucosal barrier impairment:** The mucosal barrier in the intestines, which normally prevents harmful substances from entering the bloodstream, is compromised in IBD. This allows bacteria and other antigens to cross into the intestinal tissue, triggering inflammation.

- **Tight junction proteins:** Abnormalities in tight junction proteins, crucial for maintaining the integrity of the intestinal barrier, are observed in IBD patients, leading to increased intestinal permeability

4.7. Immunodeficiency disorders

- **Primary immunodeficiencies:** Certain rare primary immunodeficiency disorders, such as Chronic Granulomatous Disease, increase susceptibility to severe, early-onset IBD due to impaired immune responses against infections and dysregulated inflammation.

4.8. Psychosocial factors

- **Stress and mental health:** While not a direct cause, stress and psychological factors can exacerbate IBD symptoms. Chronic stress might influence the immune system and gut motility, worsening disease activity.

5. Pathogenesis

5.1. Immunological dysregulation

An aberrant immune response involving the innate and adaptive immune systems is what defines inflammatory bowel disease (IBD). When innate immune cells—like dendritic and macrophage cells—are improperly activated, proinflammatory cytokines are released.

5.2. T-Cell activation

In CD and UC, there is a breakdown in tolerance to the gut microbiota or antigens. This triggers the activation of CD4+ T-cells.Th1 cells dominate the immune response in CD, while Th2 cells are more prevalent in UC.T-cell migration to the gut is facilitated by integrins and adhesion molecules.

5.3. Cytokine production

Inflammation is caused by increased levels of proinflammatory cytokines, such as interleukin-6 (IL-6), interleukin-12 (IL-12), interleukin-23 (IL-23), and tumor necrosis factor-alpha (TNF-α). These cytokines sustain tissue damage, attract immune cells to the site of inflammation, and encourage T-cell activation.

5.4. Barrier dysfunction

In IBD, the intestinal barrier function is compromised, allowing luminal antigens, such as bacterial components, to penetrate the mucosa. Tight junction proteins, like claudins and occludins, are altered, leading to increased permeability and translocation of bacteria and antigens.

5.5. Microbiota dysbiosis

IBD patients have an unbalanced composition of gut microbiota. A reduction in helpful bacteria (like Firmicutes) and an increase in potentially harmful bacteria (like Proteobacteria) characterize dysbiosis. This dysbiosis sustains inflammation and aids in immune activation.

5.6. Epithelial cell damage

Epithelial cells lining the gut are susceptible to damage in IBD. Epithelial apoptosis and increased cell turnover result in impaired barrier function and increased exposure to luminal antigens. Decreased production of mucin and defensins further weakens the barrier.

5.7. Neutrophil recruitment

In response to chemotactic signals like IL-8, neutrophils are quickly drawn to the site of inflammation. Tissue damage is exacerbated by neutrophils, which also release mediators of inflammation.

5.8. Formation of granulomas (CD)

Granulomas may develop as a result of transmural inflammation in Crohn's disease. Granulomas are a characteristic feature of CD pathology that are collections of immune cells, mainly T-cells and macrophages.

5.9. Vascular changes

Chronic inflammation in the gut causes changes in the blood vessels, leading to angiogenesis and increased vascular permeability. These vascular changes sustain the inflammatory process.

5.10. Extraintestinal manifestations

IBD can manifest outside the gastrointestinal tract, affecting various systems, including the skin, joints, liver, and eyes. This suggests systemic immune dysregulation.

5.11. Chronicity and fibrosis

IBD is characterized by a chronic and relapsing course. Repeated episodes of inflammation can lead to fibrotic changes, strictures, and loss of normal tissue architecture.

6. Sign and symptoms

6.1. General symptoms

- **Chronic Diarrhea:** Frequent and loose bowel movements.
- **Abdominal Pain:** Cramping and discomfort in the abdominal area.
- **Weight Loss:** Unintentional weight loss due to malabsorption and reduced appetite.

6.2. Specific symptoms for crohn's disease

- **Mouth Sores:** Ulcers in the mouth.
- **Perianal Disease:** Fistulas, abscesses, and pain in the anal area.
- **Skip Lesions:** Discontinuous areas of inflammation throughout the digestive tract.
- **Nutritional Deficiencies:** Due to malabsorption, leading to anemia, fatigue, and vitamin deficiencies.
- **Extraintestinal Manifestations:** Joint pain, skin rashes, and eye problems.

6.3. Specific symptoms for ulcerative colitis

- **Bloody Diarrhea:** Diarrhea with visible blood.
- **Tenesmus:** The constant feeling of needing to have a bowel movement.

- **Urgency:** Sudden, strong urges to have a bowel movement.
- **Rectal Bleeding:** Blood in the rectal area.
- **Left-Sided Abdominal Pain:** Pain on the left side of the abdomen.
- **Toxic Megacolon:** A rare and potentially fatal condition marked by extreme colon dilatation and inflammation.

6.4. Common symptoms for both crohn's disease and ulcerative colitis

- **Fatigue:** Due to chronic inflammation and anemia.
- **Fever:** An elevated body temperature often associated with disease flares.
- **Reduced Appetite:** Loss of appetite and difficulty eating.
- **Joint Pain:** Arthralgia and joint swelling.
- **Skin Issues:** Erythema nodosum and pyoderma gangrenosum.
- **Eye Inflammation:** Uveitis and scleritis.
- **Growth Failure (in Children):** Slowed growth and delayed puberty.

7. Diagnosis

A combination of clinical assessment, laboratory testing, endoscopic evaluation, imaging studies, and histopathological analysis is usually used to diagnose inflammatory bowel disease (IBD). An extensive description of the IBD diagnostic procedure is provided below, along with a list of particular tests:

7.1. Clinical assessment

A thorough medical history, including the duration and nature of symptoms, family history of IBD, and extraintestinal manifestations, is obtained.

7.2. Physical examination

The healthcare provider performs a physical examination to assess general health and identify signs such as abdominal tenderness and growth failure (in children).

7.3. Blood tests

A panel of blood tests is commonly ordered, including:

- **Complete Blood Count (CBC):** To check for anemia and elevated white blood cell count.
- **C-Reactive Protein and Erythrocyte Sedimentation Rate :** To assess inflammation.
- **Serum Albumin and Total Protein:** To evaluate nutritional status.
- **Serum Iron Studies (Ferritin, Iron, Transferrin):** To assess iron status.
- **Anti-Saccharomyces cerevisiae Antibodies (ASCA):** Elevated levels may suggest Crohn's disease.
- **Anti-Neutrophil Cytoplasmic Antibodies (ANCA):** Positive results may indicate Ulcerative Colitis.

7.4. Stool tests

Stool samples are collected and analyzed for:

- **Fecal Calprotectin:** Elevated levels indicate intestinal inflammation.
- **Fecal Blood:** Detects occult blood, indicative of gastrointestinal bleeding.
- **Stool Culture and Ova and Parasite (O&P) Examination:** To rule out infections and parasitic infestations.

7.5. Imaging studies

Radiological imaging helps visualize the gastrointestinal tract. Common imaging methods include:

- **Colonoscopy:** Direct visualization of the colon and rectum, with biopsies taken for histological assessment.
- **Upper Endoscopy:** Examination of the upper gastrointestinal tract.
- **CT Scan and MRI:** To identify inflammation, strictures, and complications.
- **Barium X-ray:** Uses contrast to visualize the digestive tract.

7.6. Capsule endoscopy

Involves swallowing a camera-equipped capsule in order to take pictures of the small intestine that may not be possible to obtain with a colonoscopy or standard endoscopy.

7.7. Genetic testing

Identifies specific genetic markers associated with IBD susceptibility, such as NOD2 variants.

7.8. Histopathological analysis

Biopsy samples taken during endoscopy or colonoscopy are examined under a microscope to assess tissue inflammation, the presence of granulomas (associated with Crohn's disease), and the extent of damage.

8. Management

A comprehensive strategy to care is necessary for Inflammatory Bowel Disease (IBD), which includes Crohn's disease (CD) and Ulcerative Colitis (UC). Remission induction and maintenance, quality of life enhancement, avoidance of problems, and therapy side effect minimization are the objectives. Management strategies involve lifestyle modifications, pharmacological interventions, surgical options, and psychological support.

8.1. Lifestyle modifications

8.1.1. Dietary Management

- **Balanced Diet:** Stress eating a diet high in fruits, vegetables, and whole grains that is well-balanced and easily digested. If you are lactose intolerant, limit processed foods and dairy.

- **Food Diary:** Patients may keep a food diary to identify trigger foods and avoid them.

- **Special Diets:** Some patients benefit from low-residue, low-FODMAP, or specific carbohydrate diets.

8.1.2. Stress management

- **Relaxation Techniques:** Promote stress-relieving activities like yoga, meditation, and deep breathing.

- **Counselling:** Offer counselling and support to manage stress and anxiety, which can exacerbate symptoms.

- **Smoking Cessation:** Strongly advise and support patients to quit smoking, especially for CD patients where smoking worsens the condition.

8.2. Pharmacological interventions

- **Aminosalicylates (5-ASAs):** Suitable for mild to moderate UC and CD affecting the colon. Examples include mesalamine and sulfasalazine.

- **Corticosteroids:** Short-term use to induce remission in moderate to severe flares. Prednisone and budesonide are common choices.

- **Immunomodulators:** Azathioprine, 6-mercaptopurine, and methotrexate for maintenance therapy in moderate to severe cases.

- **Biologic Therapies:** Anti-TNF agents (infliximab, adalimumab), anti-integrin agents (vedolizumab), and interleukin inhibitors (ustekinumab) for moderate to severe refractory cases.

- **JAK Inhibitors:** Tofacitinib for patients who have failed other treatments.

- **Antibiotics:** Metronidazole and ciprofloxacin in specific situations, such as perianal disease in CD.

8.3. Surgical options

- **Strictureplasty:** For CD patients with strictures, this surgery widens narrowed areas of the intestine, preserving healthy tissue.

- **Resection:** Removal of diseased segments of the intestine.

- **Colectomy:** In cases of severe UC or complications, removing the colon and rectum may be necessary.

- **Ileostomy or colostomy:** Creating a stoma for the elimination of waste in cases of extensive bowel removal.

8.4. Monitoring and preventive measures

- **Regular follow-ups:** Schedule regular check-ups to monitor disease activity, medication efficacy, and potential side effects.

- **Vaccinations:** Make sure patients have received all recommended vaccinations, particularly those for pneumococcal and influenza due to increased susceptibility.

- **Bone health:** Monitor and supplement calcium and vitamin D to counteract the bone-thinning effects of corticosteroids.

- **Cancer screening:** Regular surveillance for colorectal cancer, especially in long-standing UC patients.

8.5. Psychological support

- **Support groups:** Encourage participation in IBD support groups, providing a platform for sharing experiences and coping strategies.

- **Therapy:** Cognitive-behavioral therapy (CBT) and counselling can help manage stress and improve mental well-being.

- **Patient education:** Provide resources and education about IBD, its management, and coping strategies.

9. Prevention

9.1. Diet and nutrition

- Balanced Diet: Consume a well-balanced diet rich in fruits, vegetables, and whole grains.

- Limit Processed Foods: Reduce the intake of processed and high-sugar foods.

- Omega-3 Fatty Acids: Incorporate anti-inflammatory foods high in omega-3 fatty acids, such as walnuts, flaxseeds, and fish.

9.2. Smoking cessation

In particular, if you are at risk or have a family history of IBD, give up smoking. One major cause of risk for Crohn's disease is smoking.

9.3. Probiotics

Consider the use of probiotics to maintain a healthy gut microbiota balance. However, consult a healthcare provider before starting any supplements.

9.4. Breastfeeding

Encourage breastfeeding in infants, as it may reduce the risk of developing IBD.

9.5. Hygiene

Practice good hygiene to reduce the risk of gastrointestinal infections that may trigger IBD.

9.6. Reduce stress

Practice stress-relieving methods such as yoga, meditation, and deep breathing.

9.7. Non-steroidal anti-Inflammatory drugs (NSAIDs)

Use NSAIDs, such as ibuprofen and aspirin, cautiously, as they may exacerbate IBD or trigger its onset in susceptible individuals.

9.8. Early treatment of infections

Promptly treat gastrointestinal infections to prevent potential complications or the development of chronic inflammation.

9.9. Genetic counselling

If you have a family history of IBD, consider genetic counselling to assess your risk and take appropriate measures.

9.10. Environmental exposures

Minimize exposure to environmental toxins and pollutants, as there is some evidence suggesting they may be associated with IBD.

10. Conclusions

Both Crohn's disease (CD) and ulcerative colitis (UC) are chronic gastrointestinal disorders that are becoming more common worldwide. These disorders are known as inflammatory bowel disease (IBD). Genetic predisposition, immunological dysregulation, environmental factors, microbiota imbalance, and other factors are all part of its intricate etiology. Managing IBD requires a multifaceted approach, including lifestyle changes, medication, surgery, monitoring, and psychological support. Prevention strategies involve dietary choices, smoking cessation, probiotics, breastfeeding, hygiene, stress reduction, cautious NSAID use, early infection treatment, genetic counseling, and environmental awareness. Consulting healthcare professionals and current medical literature is essential for accurate and up-to-date information.

References

1. Baumgart, D. C., & Sandborn, W. J. (2012). Inflammatory bowel disease: clinical aspects and established and evolving therapies. The Lancet, 380(9851), 1590-1605.
2. Torres, J., Mehandru, S., Colombel, J. F., &Peyrin-Biroulet, L. (2017). Crohn's disease. The Lancet, 389(10080), 1741-1755.
3. Ungaro, R., Mehandru, S., Allen, P. B., Peyrin-Biroulet, L., & Colombel, J. F. (2017). Ulcerative colitis. The Lancet, 389(10080), 1756-1770.
4. Ananthakrishnan, A. N., Bernstein, C. N., Iliopoulos, D., Macpherson, A., Neurath, M. F., & Ali, R. (2018). Environmental triggers in IBD: a review of progress and evidence. Nature Reviews Gastroenterology & Hepatology, 15(1), 39-49.
5. Khor, B., Gardet, A., & Xavier, R. J. (2011). Genetics and pathogenesis of inflammatory bowel disease. Nature, 474(7351), 307-317.
6. Neurath, M. F. (2014). Cytokines in inflammatory bowel disease. Nature Reviews Immunology, 14(5), 329-342.
7. Xavier, R. J., & Podolsky, D. K. (2007). Unravelling the pathogenesis of inflammatory bowel disease. Nature, 448(7152), 427-434.
8. Kaser, A., Zeissig, S., & Blumberg, R. S. (2010). Inflammatory bowel disease. Annual Review of Immunology, 28, 573-621.

9. Feuerstein, J. D., Cheifetz, A. S., &Raffals, L. E. (2019). Overview of epidemiology, pathogenesis, and diagnosis of inflammatory bowel disease. Inflammatory Bowel Diseases, 25(5), 742-753.

10. Danese, S., & Fiocchi, C. (2011). Ulcerative colitis. New England Journal of Medicine, 365(18), 1713-1725.

2.

Prevention of Inflammatory Bowel Disease (IBD)

Dr. Prof. Gopeswar Mukherjee

M.B.B.S., D.C.P & M.D(Path), Ph.D.

(Path) Professor & Dean,

Brainware University, Kolkata

Email: mukherjeeclinicallab@gmail.com

Abstract

Prevention of irritable bowel disease (IBD) involves adopting certain lifestyle modifications and managing risk factors to reduce the likelihood of developing the condition. IBD refers to a group of chronic inflammatory bowel diseases, including Crohn's disease and ulcerative colitis, which result in inflammation of the intestines. One key aspect of prevention is maintaining a healthy diet. Consuming a balanced, high-fiber diet can help regulate bowel movements and reduce the risk of developing IBD. Avoiding trigger foods, such as fatty or fried foods, spicy foods, and dairy products, may also be helpful in preventing symptoms. Regular exercise has been linked to a reduced risk of IBD. Physical activity helps maintain a healthy weight, improves digestive health, and strengthens the immune system, all of which can contribute to preventing IBD.

Managing stress is another important preventive measure. Chronic stress has been associated with an increased risk of IBD. Practicing stress-reducing techniques, such as mindfulness, yoga, or meditation, can help prevent the onset of the disease. Avoiding smoking and limiting alcohol consumption are also crucial in preventing IBD. Both smoking and excessive alcohol intake have been linked to an increased risk of developing the condition. Additionally, maintaining a healthy gut microbiome is key in preventing IBD. Consuming probiotics, which are beneficial bacteria found in certain foods or supplements, may help maintain a healthy balance of gut bacteria and reduce inflammation. It is important to consult a healthcare professional for personalized advice on prevention strategies based on individual risk factors. While these preventative measures may not guarantee full prevention of IBD, they can significantly reduce the likelihood of developing the condition.

1. Introduction

Inflammatory bowel disease is a term used to describe a set of inflammatory conditions that affect the colon and small intestine. The primary conditions are Crohn's disease and ulcerative colitis. Crohn's disease typically affects the small and large intestines, as well as the mouth, stomach, and anus, whereas ulcerative colitis mostly affects the colon and rectum.

2. Causes

IBD is a complicated illness caused by the combination of hereditary and environmental factors, culminating in an immune response and inflammation in the gut.

2.1. Diet

Fried and spicy foods should be avoided. They should consume more veggies. Reduce your consumption of processed meats and refined carbohydrates. Gluten sensitivity is frequent in IBD and is linked to flare-ups. High protein, particularly animal protein, and/or high sugar diets should be avoided.

2.2. Breach of the intestinal barrier

The integrity of the intestinal epithelium is compromised in IBD. Detrimental alterations in the intestinal microbiota can result in an incorrect amount of response, which can cause damage to the intestinal epithelium, allowing the immune response to continue. IBD is a multifactorial disease. IBD pathogenesis is thought to be influenced by oxidative stress and DNA damage. Oxidative DNA damage, as evaluated by 8 - OHDG levels, was shown to be considerably higher in IBD patients compared to controls.

2.3. Genetic

For over a century, people have suspected that IBD has a genetic component. The genes linked to IBD are likely to be linked to anxiety, depression, and so on. Patients with IBD have complications from both the disease and the immunosuppressive medicines used to treat it.

Primary, secondary, and tertiary prevention of IBD must all be considered.

Essential anticipation is defined as the prevention of sickness progression. Immunization against infectious illnesses is one example of primary prevention, as is educational intervention such as regular exercise. This can happen at the individual or population level. One example is primary prevention with water fluoridation, which leads to the prevention of dental cavities. Different forms of vaccinations, such as influenza and pneumococcal pneumonia, are also noted.

HPV vaccination has been found to protect against particular HPV serotypes. Another approach to primary prevention of IBD is the use of sunscreen to prevent skin cancer, which has been shown to increase disease severity in IBD patients. Weight-bearing activities and calcium/vitamin supplements, when needed, help to avoid osteoporotic gynecomastia in IBD patients who may require steroid treatments in the future.

3. Secondary prevention

Secondary prevention is described as detective work done to avoid abnormalities as such through screening programs. As a result, there is a high need for secondary prevention in IBD patients. Patients with IBD, for example, have an elevated risk of Melanoma. Individuals on anti-TNF medications have a twofold increased risk of getting melanoma.

As a result, the Dermatologist skin cleansing program is advised for all IBD patients. Previously, it was indicated that individuals with IBD who were on immune suppression had a higher risk of abnormal pap smears and/or cervical dyspepsia. In patients with IBD who are immunocompromised, a yearly cervical skin check is advised. Patients with IBD who have had a long-standing colonic for more than ten years are more likely to develop colorectal?? and cancer. As a result, individuals with chronic colonic inflammation should be evaluated.

4. Tertiary prevention

Tertiary prevention refers to steps taken to lessen the impact of long-term disease and disabilities on? chronic disease of ongoing inflammation can lead to the formation of stricture, which can produce blockages and necessitate surgery. It can sometimes result in the formation of a fistula, which is an improper connection between two organs that can result in an abscess and other issues. In the event of arthritis colitis, ongoing inflammation may raise the risk of colon cancer and dysplasia. Thus, illness can sometimes cause exclusively left-side involvement over time. We can reduce morbidity and even life-threatening consequences of IBD by treating this inflammation early with the objective of mucosal repair. Each IBD patient should be evaluated regularly by both a primary care physician and a specialist. This proactive approach to IBD prevention, which addresses primary, secondary, and tertiary prevention, can eventually assist in minimizing infections, malignancies, and long-term consequences. In reality, each IBD patient requires community assistance. A care plan for each IBD patient may be executed through teamwork. Considering his or her own needs and aspirations. As a result, three types of prevention are implemented: primary, secondary, and tertiary. The lives of IBD patients can be improved.

5. Preventive interventions for IBD

1. Quitting smoking
2. Physical activities and exercise
3. Proper nutrition
4. Anemia screening
5. Bone health maintenance and prevention of osteoporotic and osteopenic alterations.
6. Eye health
7. Latent infection screening
8. Vaccination
9. Sleep disorder screening
10. Mental health
11. Cardiovascular health
12. To avoid steroid overuse
13. Cancer screening for cervical cancer, skin cancer, colorectal cancer, breast cancer, and prostate cancer
14. Preventive health care can lower morbidity, morale, and total costs

6. Conclusions

In conclusion, taking preventive measures is crucial in managing and preventing irritable bowel disorder. By adopting a healthy lifestyle, managing stress, implementing dietary changes, and seeking medical advice, individuals can significantly reduce the risk of developing this condition. It is important to remember that each person's experience with irritable bowel syndrome is unique, and finding the right approach may require some trial and error. With determination and proper care, individuals can lead a fulfilling and comfortable life, free from the symptoms of irritable bowel disorder.

References

1. Kaplan GG. Ng Sc. Understanding and preventing the Global Increase of Inflammatory Bowel Disease. Gastroenterology 2017, 152:313-321.e2.

2. Weaver KN, Long MD. Preventive Medicine in Inflammatory Bowel Disease. Clin Gastroenterol Hepatol 2019, 17 : 824-828.

3. Long MD, Martin C, Sandler RS, et al. Increased risk of case Am J Gastroenterol 2013:108:240-8.

4. Winthrop KL, Melmed GY, Vermeire S, et al. Herpes Zoster Infection in Patients. With Ulcerative Colitis Receiving Tofacitinib. Inflamin Bowel Dis 2018:24:2285-2265.

5. Long MD, Martin CF, Pipkin CA, et al. Risk of melanoma and nonmelanoma skin cancer among patients with inflammatory bowel disease. Gastroenterology 2012:143;390-399:el.

6. Kane S. Khatibi B. Reddy D. Higher incidence of abnormal Pap smears in women with

inflammatory bowel disease. Am J Gastroenterol 2008; 103:631-6.

7. Peyrin-Biroulet L, Sandborn W, Sands BE, et al. Selecting Therapeutic Targets in Inflammatory Bowel disease (STRIDF) : Determining Therapeutic Goals for Treat-to-Target. Am J Gastroenterol 2015:110:1324-38.

3.

Quality of Life of Inflammatory Bowel Disease Patients

Baijnath Das[1], Shivam Agarwal[1], Dr. (Prof.) Navneet Kumar[3*]

[1]Assistant Professor, [2]Vice Principal

Teerthanker Mahaveer University College of Paramedical Sciences, Moradabad[1].

Email: baijnathdasbiochemaiims@gmail.com

Email: shivamagarwal50283@gmail.com

Email: Navneet.paramedical@gmail.com

Abstract

Inflammatory Bowel Disease (IBD), encompassing Crohn's disease and ulcerative colitis, is a chronic condition significantly impacting millions worldwide. This chapter explores the multifaceted dimensions of the quality of life in IBD patients. Assessing quality of life is essential due to the lifelong nature of IBD and its wide-ranging impact beyond health. The chapter examines the physical, emotional, and social implications of IBD, emphasizing the importance of tailored assessment tools. Factors affecting quality of life are discussed, including disease type, comorbidities, socioeconomic status, social support, and more. Effective treatment approaches encompass medications, surgery, dietary considerations, and a holistic approach.

Psychosocial support plays a vital role, addressing coping, stigma, and community resources. Nutritional considerations are explored, highlighting the role of diet in symptom management. The chapter concludes with future directions in IBD care, emphasizing personalized medicine and advocacy. Recommendations for improving quality of life encompass multidisciplinary care, patient empowerment, mental health support, and addressing stigma. Incorporating these recommendations into IBD care ensures a patient-centered, holistic approach, enhancing overall well-being.

Keywords: IBD, Quality of life, Psychosocial, Nutrition, Future directions, Recommendations.

1. Introduction

Inflammatory Bowel Disease (IBD), encompassing both Crohn's disease and ulcerative colitis, is a chronic and often debilitating condition that affects millions of individuals worldwide. Characterized by chronic inflammation of the gastrointestinal tract, IBD significantly impacts not only the physical health but also the overall well-being of those diagnosed. In this chapter, we delve into the multifaceted dimensions of the quality of life experienced by individuals living with IBD.

1.1. Significance of assessing quality of life in IBD patients

Understanding the quality of life in IBD patients is of paramount importance for several reasons. Firstly, IBD is a lifelong condition, typically diagnosed in early adulthood, and can persist for decades. As a result, patients must adapt to the chronicity of their illness and cope with a range of physical and emotional challenges throughout their lives. Secondly, the impact of IBD extends beyond the immediate health concerns, affecting the patients' education, employment, relationships, and overall life satisfaction. Therefore, assessing the quality of life offers insights into the broader implications of IBD on the well-being of those affected.

2. Assessing the impact of IBD on quality of life

Inflammatory Bowel Disease (IBD) is a complex chronic condition that exacts a profound toll on the quality of life of those affected. To better understand the impact of IBD, it is imperative to examine the diverse dimensions through which it affects the overall well-being of patients.

2.1. Physical symptoms and limitations

One of the most overt ways in which IBD impairs quality of life is through its array of physical symptoms. Abdominal pain, diarrhea, rectal bleeding, fatigue, and weight loss are common symptoms that can be debilitating. These physical symptoms often result in limitations in daily activities, work, and social engagements. For some, severe IBD flares may lead to hospitalization, surgery, or temporary disability, making it challenging to maintain a regular life routine.

2.2. Emotional and psychological challenges

The emotional and psychological aspects of living with IBD are equally significant. The chronic nature of the disease, the unpredictability of symptom flares, and the necessity of managing symptoms and treatments can lead to stress, anxiety, and depression. Patients may experience a sense of loss, both of physical health and the life they once knew. The psychological impact of IBD extends beyond the individual patient to family members and caregivers who are often deeply affected.

2.3. Social and interpersonal implications

IBD can disrupt social relationships and limit social activities. Individuals living with IBD may face challenges related to stigma, as discussing gastrointestinal symptoms and bathroom needs can be uncomfortable and stigmatizing in social settings. The need for frequent bathroom visits or dietary restrictions can lead to feelings of isolation. Relationships, including those with family, friends, and colleagues, may be strained as patients cope with the demands of the disease.

2.4. Quantitative and qualitative measurement tools

To assess the impact of IBD on quality of life, various quantitative and qualitative measurement tools have been developed. These tools include disease-specific questionnaires and surveys that evaluate the physical, emotional, and social dimensions of quality of life in IBD patients. They can help healthcare providers and researchers gain insight into the patient's experience and monitor changes over time. Qualitative methods, such as interviews and narratives, provide a more in-depth understanding of the lived experience of IBD patients, shedding light on their coping strategies and challenges.

3. Factors affecting quality of life in IBD patients

The quality of life for individuals living with Inflammatory Bowel Disease (IBD) is influenced by a multitude of factors that extend beyond the disease itself. Recognizing and understanding these factors is essential for providing comprehensive care and support to IBD patients.

3.1. Disease severity and type (crohn's disease vs. ulcerative colitis)

The type and severity of IBD play a significant role in determining a patient's quality of life. Crohn's disease and ulcerative colitis, while both forms of IBD, exhibit distinct characteristics. Crohn's disease can affect any part of the gastrointestinal tract and often leads to complications like strictures and fistulas. Ulcerative colitis, on the other hand, primarily affects the colon and rectum. The different locations and complications associated with these conditions can result in varying symptoms, treatment approaches, and quality-of-life impacts.

3.2. Comorbidities and complications

Many IBD patients experience comorbidities (co-occurring medical conditions) and complications, which further affect their quality of life. These may include arthritis, skin problems, liver conditions, and eye disorders. Additionally, complications such as abscesses, blockages, and perforations can lead to hospitalizations and surgeries, significantly impacting a patient's daily life and overall well-being.

3.3. Socioeconomic status

Socioeconomic status can exert a substantial influence on the quality of life for IBD patients. Access to healthcare, including medications and specialized treatments, can vary based on financial resources and insurance coverage. Employment and financial stability are often jeopardized due to frequent medical appointments, hospitalizations, and unpredictable symptom flares. Patients with limited financial resources may face added stress and uncertainty regarding their ability to afford the necessary care and support.

3.4. Social support and relationships

Social support is a key determinant of quality of life for IBD patients. Having a strong support system, including understanding family and friends, can help patients cope with the emotional and practical challenges of the disease. Conversely, a lack of social support can contribute to feelings of isolation and despair. Relationships may be strained due to the demands of

IBD, and some patients may face challenges in disclosing their condition to others.

3.5. Geographic location

Geographic location can influence the quality of life for IBD patients. Access to specialized healthcare facilities, experienced healthcare providers, and clinical trials may vary depending on where a patient lives. Rural or remote areas may have limited access to IBD care, leading to delays in diagnosis and treatment.

3.6. Age at diagnosis

The age at which IBD is diagnosed can impact a patient's quality of life. Pediatric patients, for example, face unique challenges related to growth, development, and education. Young adults may confront obstacles in establishing their careers and independence. Older adults diagnosed with IBD may have different concerns, such as comorbidities or managing the disease alongside age-related health issues.

3.7. Gender and reproductive health

Gender can also play a role in how IBD affects quality of life. Women with IBD may experience unique challenges related to pregnancy, childbirth, and hormonal fluctuations. Men may face concerns related to fertility and sexual health. These gender-specific issues can influence overall well-being and should be considered in the management of IBD.

3.8. Disease activity and flares

The frequency and intensity of disease flares and periods of remission significantly impact an IBD patient's quality of life. Frequent and severe flares can disrupt daily routines, work, and social activities. The unpredictability of flares can lead to anxiety and distress, affecting emotional well-being.

3.9. Medication side effects

The medications used to manage IBD can have side effects, which can vary from patient to patient. Some individuals may experience side effects that impact their quality of life, such as weight gain, mood swings, or increased susceptibility to infections. Balancing the benefits of medications with potential side effects is a crucial consideration.

3.10. Patient resilience and coping mechanisms

Individual differences in coping mechanisms and resilience can affect how IBD patients adapt to and manage the disease. Some patients may have strong coping strategies and adapt well to the challenges of IBD, leading to better quality of life. Others may struggle to cope with the emotional and physical demands of the condition.

3.11. Cultural and socioeconomic background

Cultural and socioeconomic factors can influence how IBD is perceived and managed. Cultural beliefs, dietary preferences, and healthcare-seeking behaviors may differ among individuals, impacting their approach to treatment and quality of life. Socioeconomic factors, including education and employment opportunities, can also shape a patient's experience.

3.12. Mental health history

A history of pre-existing mental health conditions, such as anxiety or depression, can intersect with IBD and influence an individual's quality of life. Patients with a history of mental health issues may be more vulnerable to emotional distress when dealing with IBD.

4. Treatment approaches and quality of life improvement

Improving the quality of life for individuals living with Inflammatory Bowel Disease (IBD) is a multifaceted endeavour that involves both medical and psychosocial approaches. The management of IBD aims not only to control the disease's activity but also to enhance the overall well-being of patients.

4.1. Medications and therapies

Pharmaceutical interventions are a cornerstone of IBD management. Medications such as anti-inflammatory drugs, immunosuppressants, and biologics are employed to control disease activity and reduce inflammation. The appropriate selection and administration of these medications are crucial in preventing flares and maintaining remission. Effective medication management can lead to symptom relief, improved energy levels, and enhanced quality of life.

4.2. Surgery and its impact

In some cases, surgical intervention becomes necessary, especially for patients with complications like strictures, fistulas, or uncontrolled bleeding. Surgical procedures such as bowel resections can alleviate symptoms and improve the overall well-being of patients. However, surgery can also present challenges, such as recovery periods and potential changes in bowel habits, which must be managed to optimize the patient's quality of life.

4.3. Diet and nutrition

Diet and nutrition play a significant role in managing IBD and improving the quality of life. Patients often experience dietary triggers and intolerances that exacerbate symptoms. By working with dietitians and nutritionists, individuals can identify trigger foods and develop customized diets that reduce symptom flares and promote overall health. Nutritional supplements may be necessary to address deficiencies and enhance well-being.

4.4. Role of healthcare providers

The expertise and support provided by healthcare providers are integral to IBD management. Gastroenterologists, nurses, and other specialists work together to ensure appropriate monitoring and care. Regular follow-up appointments, timely adjustments to treatment plans, and proactive management of side effects are essential to maintaining the patient's quality of life.

5. Psychosocial support and quality of life improvement

In addition to medical interventions, psychosocial strategies are crucial for enhancing the quality of life for IBD patients.

5.1. Family and caregiver support

The involvement of family members and caregivers is invaluable in improving a patient's quality of life. They can offer emotional support, help manage daily activities, and assist with medication adherence. Education and awareness programs for families can enhance their understanding of IBD and improve the patient's overall support system.

5.2. Peer support and community resources

Peer support, often provided through patient advocacy groups and online communities, offers individuals an opportunity to connect with others facing similar challenges. These support networks provide valuable insights, shared experiences, and a sense of belonging that can positively impact the patient's quality of life.

5.3. Education and awareness programs

Education and awareness programs for patients, families, and the general public are essential in reducing the stigma associated with IBD and promoting understanding. Greater awareness can lead to increased support, improved social interactions, and enhanced quality of life for IBD patients.

6. Psychosocial and emotional aspects of living with IBD

Inflammatory Bowel Disease (IBD) is not merely a physical ailment; it has significant psychosocial and emotional implications that affect the overall well-being of individuals with the condition. Understanding these aspects is essential for providing comprehensive care and support to IBD patients.

6.1. Coping mechanisms

Living with IBD requires effective coping mechanisms to navigate the emotional and psychological challenges that arise. Patients often experience anxiety, depression, fear, and frustration, especially during symptom flares and periods of uncertainty. Coping strategies can include mindfulness techniques, relaxation exercises, and stress-reduction methods. Engaging in hobbies, physical activity, or creative outlets can also provide a healthy distraction from the challenges of the disease.

6.2. Anxiety and depression

Anxiety and depression are common psychological challenges for IBD patients. The chronic and unpredictable nature of the disease, coupled with its impact on daily life, can lead to persistent feelings of anxiety and sadness. These emotions can affect the patient's overall quality of life, as they may withdraw from social activities and become increasingly isolated.

6.3. Stigma and disclosure

Stigma associated with IBD can be a significant psychological burden. Due to the nature of gastrointestinal symptoms, patients may feel embarrassed or uncomfortable discussing their condition with others. Fear of judgment or misconceptions about IBD can lead to secrecy, withdrawal, and avoidance of social situations, resulting in a diminished quality of life.

6.4. Support groups and counselling

Psychosocial support is essential for addressing the emotional aspects of living with IBD. Support groups, either in person or online, can offer individuals the opportunity to connect with others facing similar challenges. These groups provide a safe space to share experiences, receive advice, and find emotional support.

Counselling, either individually or as part of a family or caregiver network, can be instrumental in helping IBD patients cope with the emotional impact of the disease. Professional counselling can provide strategies for managing anxiety and depression, as well as improving communication and relationships with loved ones.

7. Nutritional considerations and quality of life

Nutrition plays a pivotal role in the management of Inflammatory Bowel Disease (IBD) and can have a profound impact on the quality of life of individuals living with the condition. Nutritional considerations are essential for symptom control, overall well-being, and long-term health.

7.1. Managing gastrointestinal symptoms

IBD patients often experience gastrointestinal symptoms such as abdominal pain, diarrhea, and bloating. Certain foods and dietary patterns can exacerbate these symptoms. Identifying trigger foods and making appropriate dietary adjustments can lead to symptom relief and improved quality of life. Healthcare providers often recommend keeping a food diary to track symptoms in relation to dietary choices.

7.2. Nutritional deficiencies

Malabsorption and inflammation in the gastrointestinal tract can lead to nutritional deficiencies in IBD patients. Deficits in essential vitamins and minerals, such as vitamin D, vitamin B12, iron, and calcium, can impact overall health and well-being. Regular monitoring of nutritional status and the use of supplements or dietary modifications can mitigate deficiencies and improve the patient's quality of life.

7.3. Special diets for IBD

Some IBD patients may benefit from special diets tailored to their specific needs. For example, the low-FODMAP diet, which reduces fermentable carbohydrates, can be useful in managing symptoms in some patients. The Specific Carbohydrate Diet (SCD) and the Crohn's Disease Exclusion Diet (CDED) are other specialized diets that have been explored for their potential to improve quality of life in IBD patients.

7.4. Managing gastrointestinal symptoms

IBD patients often experience gastrointestinal symptoms such as abdominal pain, diarrhea, and bloating. Certain foods and dietary patterns can exacerbate these symptoms. Identifying trigger foods and making appropriate dietary adjustments can lead to symptom relief and improved quality of life. Healthcare providers often recommend keeping a food diary to track symptoms in relation to dietary choices.

7.5. Tailoring nutrition to the individual

Each IBD patient is unique, and their dietary needs may vary. Healthcare providers, often in collaboration with registered dietitians, work with patients to develop personalized dietary plans. These plans take into account the patient's specific symptoms, nutritional deficiencies, and preferences, ensuring that they receive the necessary nutrients to support their overall health and quality of life.

7.6. Holistic approach to diet and nutrition

A holistic approach to diet and nutrition in IBD management considers not only the physical aspects of nutrition but also the psychosocial components. Coping with dietary restrictions and managing social aspects of food can be challenging for IBD patients. Education and support for patients and their families in navigating these challenges are critical in promoting a positive relationship with food and an enhanced quality of life.

8. Future directions in enhancing quality of life for IBD patients

The landscape of care and support for individuals with Inflammatory Bowel Disease (IBD) is continually evolving, offering promising avenues for enhancing the quality of life for IBD patients. As research and medical advancements progress, several future directions are emerging:

8.1. Personalized medicine

The concept of personalized medicine is gaining momentum in the field of IBD. Advancements in genetic profiling and the microbiome are paving the way for tailored treatment approaches. Identifying the specific genetic and microbial factors contributing to an individual's IBD can lead to more precise, effective treatments with fewer side effects, ultimately improving the quality of life.

8.2. Advanced therapies and biologics

The development of advanced therapies and biologics is ongoing. These therapies aim to provide more targeted and efficient control of IBD symptoms while minimizing adverse effects. New biologic drugs are continually under investigation, offering the potential for improved long-term outcomes and a higher quality of life for patients.

8.3. Telemedicine and digital health

Telemedicine and digital health solutions are becoming integral to IBD care. These technologies allow patients to access healthcare remotely, receive timely consultations, and monitor their symptoms from the comfort of their homes. Telemedicine enhances convenience and accessibility, particularly for patients with limited mobility or in remote areas.

8.4. Advocacy and policy initiatives

The IBD community, along with advocacy groups and healthcare organizations, continues to work toward raising awareness and improving policy initiatives. These efforts aim to reduce the stigma associated with IBD, increase funding for research, and promote access to high-quality care. Advocacy and policy changes can lead to improved support, resources, and quality of life for IBD patients.

8.5. Patient-cantered care

The concept of patient-centered care remains at the forefront of IBD management. Empowering patients to actively participate in their care decisions, providing education, and involving them in treatment planning are essential aspects of enhancing the quality of life. A patient-centered approach recognizes the unique needs and preferences of each individual and tailors care accordingly.

8.6. Mental health integration

Recognizing the integral relationship between mental and physical health, the integration of mental health services into IBD care is gaining traction. Addressing anxiety, depression, and stress is vital for the overall well-being of patients. Future directions include greater emphasis on mental health support as an integral component of IBD management.

8.7. Research into long-term outcomes

Continued research into long-term outcomes is essential for understanding the effects of IBD on quality of life. Longitudinal studies and data analysis will shed light on the evolving needs of IBD patients over time, helping healthcare providers and researchers make informed decisions to enhance patient well-being.

As we move forward, the future holds promise for IBD patients. With advancements in personalized medicine, therapies, technology, advocacy, and research, the quality of life for individuals living with IBD is expected to improve. A holistic approach that addresses physical, psychological, and social aspects of the disease is pivotal in achieving these future directions and ensuring that IBD patients experience the highest possible quality of life.

9. Recommendations for improving quality of life in IBD patients

Improving the quality of life for individuals living with Inflammatory Bowel Disease (IBD) requires a comprehensive and patient-centered approach. Healthcare providers, support networks, and the IBD community can collaborate to implement the following recommendations:

9.1. Multidisciplinary healthcare teams

Collaborative care involving gastroenterologists, dietitians, mental health professionals, and other specialists is essential. A multidisciplinary approach ensures that all aspects of IBD, from symptom management to emotional well-being, are addressed.

9.2. Patient education and empowerment

Empowering IBD patients with knowledge about their condition is crucial. Patients should understand their treatment options, medications, dietary needs, and potential side effects. Education empowers patients to actively participate in their care decisions.

9.3. Personalized treatment plans

Tailoring treatment plans to the specific needs and preferences of each patient is vital. Personalized medicine, which considers genetic and microbiome factors, can lead to more effective and less burdensome treatments.

9.4. Mental health support

Integrated mental health services should be available as part of IBD care. Addressing anxiety, depression, and stress is essential for improving the overall well-being of patients. Mental health professionals can help patients develop coping strategies and provide emotional support.

9.5. Dietary guidance

Patients benefit from working with registered dietitians to identify trigger foods, manage nutritional deficiencies, and develop customized dietary plans.

Special diets, such as low-FODMAP or exclusion diets, should be considered where appropriate.

9.6. Telemedicine and digital health

Leveraging telemedicine and digital health solutions can enhance accessibility to care, particularly for patients with limited mobility or those in remote areas. These technologies should be integrated into IBD management.

9.7. Patient advocacy and policy initiatives

Support and engage in advocacy efforts to raise awareness about IBD, reduce stigma, and advocate for better access to care and research funding. Policy initiatives that prioritize the needs of IBD patients can significantly improve their quality of life.

9.8. Support groups and community resources

Encourage patients to join support groups, both in person and online, to connect with others facing similar challenges. These networks provide valuable emotional support, shared experiences, and a sense of belonging.

9.9. Long-term outcomes research

Support and participate in long-term outcomes research to better understand the evolving needs of IBD patients. This data can inform future care and interventions.

9.10. Holistic care

Recognize that IBD management should encompass not only physical symptoms but also psychosocial aspects. Holistic care addresses the whole person, considering emotional well-being, relationships, and overall quality of life.

9.11. Family and caregiver education

Educate family members and caregivers about IBD to enhance their understanding and ability to provide support. Informed and empathetic support networks contribute to the well-being of IBD patients.

9.12. Stigma reduction

Work collectively to reduce stigma surrounding IBD through education and awareness. Reducing misconceptions and judgment fosters a more supportive and understanding environment for patients.

Incorporating these recommendations into IBD care can lead to significant improvements in the quality of life for those living with the condition. A patient-centered and holistic approach ensures that the unique needs and preferences of each individual are addressed, ultimately enhancing their well-being and overall quality of life.

10. Conclusions

In conclusion, Inflammatory Bowel Disease (IBD) significantly impacts the physical, emotional, and social well-being of affected individuals. Disease severity, comorbidities, socioeconomic status, and various psychosocial factors all play pivotal roles in shaping the quality of life for IBD patients. Treatment approaches encompass medication, surgery, dietary management, and psychosocial support. Recognizing the emotional and psychological aspects of living with IBD, as well as addressing factors such as anxiety, depression, and stigma, is essential. Promising future directions include personalized medicine, advanced therapies, telemedicine, advocacy, and mental health integration, while recommendations for a patient-centered, holistic approach can enhance the well-being of individuals living with IBD by addressing their unique needs and fostering a more supportive environment.

Reference:

1. Loftus, E. V. (2004). Clinical epidemiology of inflammatory bowel disease: Incidence, prevalence, and environmental influences. Gastroenterology, 126(6), 1504-1517.
2. Ananthakrishnan, A. N. (2015). Epidemiology and risk factors for IBD. Nature Reviews Gastroenterology & Hepatology, 12(4), 205-217.
3. Mowat, C., Cole, A., Windsor, A., Ahmad, T., Arnott, I., Driscoll, R., ... & Bloom, S. (2011). Guidelines for the management of inflammatory bowel disease in adults. Gut, 60(5), 571-607.
4. Bernstein, C. N., Loftus, E. V., Ng, S. C., Lakatos, P. L., & Moum, B. (2012). Hospitalisations and surgery in Crohn's disease. Gut, 61(4), 622-629.
5. Mikocka-Walus, A. A., Turnbull, D. A., Moulding, N. T., Wilson, I. G., & Andrews, J. M. (2007). Controversies surrounding the comorbidity of depression and anxiety in inflammatory bowel disease patients: a literature review. Inflammatory Bowel Diseases, 13(2), 225-234.

6. Knowles, S. R., Keefer, L., Wild, B., & Mikocka-Walus, A. (2013). Quality of life in inflammatory bowel disease: a systematic review and meta-analyses—Part I. Inflammatory Bowel Diseases, 19(3), 419-430.
7. Casati, J., & Toner, B. B. (2003). Psychosocial issues in the assessment and management of patients with inflammatory bowel disease. Inflammatory Bowel Diseases, 9(3), 181-186.
8. van der Have, M., Brakenhoff, L. K., van Erp, S. J., Kaptein, A. A., Leenders, M., & Siersema, P. D. (2017). IBD and health-related quality of life—discovering a new interrelationship. The Netherlands Journal of Medicine, 75(1), 20-27.
9. Neary, P., Nanda, K. S., Lerebours, E., & Schreiber, S. (2013). Review article: a way forward for IBD management—relate or intervene? Alimentary Pharmacology & Therapeutics, 38(10), 1224-1239.
10. Ananthakrishnan, A. N., Khalili, H., Higuchi, L. M., Bao, Y., Korzenik, J. R., & Giovannucci, E. L. (2012). Higher predicted vitamin D status is associated with reduced risk of Crohn's disease. Gastroenterology, 142(3), 482-489.

4.

Malnutrition and Inflammatory Disease

Dr. Praveen Katiyar[1], Chandan Kumar[2]

[1*]Assistant Professor, School of Health Sciences, CSJM University Kanpur.

[2]Ph.D. Scholar, School of Health Sciences, CSJM University Kanpur.

Email: drpraveenkatiyar@gmail.com

Abstract

Inflammatory Bowel Disease (IBD) is a group of chronic diseases characterized by inflammation of the gastrointestinal tract, with the two primary types being Crohn's disease and ulcerative colitis. This overview delves into the types and pathophysiology of IBD, common symptoms, and the crucial role of addressing nutritional aspects in IBD management. Nutritional considerations are vital, as individuals with IBD face an increased risk of malnutrition due to factors like inflammation, reduced appetite, malabsorption, and dietary restrictions. The link between malnutrition and IBD, its causes, and prevalence are discussed, along with the impact of malnutrition on disease severity and the overall quality of life. A comprehensive approach to IBD care is essential, involving gastroenterologists, dietitians, nurses, mental health specialists, and other healthcare professionals. Patient education and empowerment are key components in managing IBD and its nutritional challenges, including self-management and dietary choices tailored to the individual's needs. Coping with nutritional challenges, perceived stigma, and lifestyle considerations is crucial for improving the quality of life for those living with IBD.

Keywords: Chronic diseases, Crohn's disease, ulcerative colitis, malabsorption

1. Inflammatory bowel disease (IBD) Overview

Inflammatory bowel disease (IBD) is a group of chronic diseases caused by inflammation of the gastrointestinal tract. The two main types of IBD are Crohn's disease and ulcerative colitis.

1.1. Crohn's disease

Crohn's disease can affect any part of the intestine, from the mouth to the rectum, but usually affects the beginnings of the small and large bowel. It is characterized by pain that can affect all processes in the intestine, causing a "jumping pattern" between affected and unaffected areas.

Types of crohn's disease

- **Ileocolitis:** Inflammation of the small intestine and part of the large intestine or colon.

- **Ileitis:** inflammation and pain of the small intestine (ileum).

- **Gastroduodenal:** Inflammation and irritation affecting the stomach and upper part of the small intestine (duodenum).

- **Geno ileitis:** Patchy area of inflammation in the upper part of the small intestine (called jejunum).

1. 2. Ulcerative colitis

Ulcerative colitis especially affects the colon and rectum. In ulcerative colitis, inflammation usually occurs in the inner lining of the intestine, causing ulcers and pain.

2. Importance of addressing nutritional aspects in IBD

Addressing the nutritional aspects of Inflammatory Bowel Disease (IBD) is of utmost **Individuals** with IBD are at an increased risk of malnutrition due to factors important for several reasons:

- **Malnutrition risk:** such as reduced appetite, malabsorption, increased nutrient loss through diarrhea, and a restricted diet due to food intolerances.

- **Inflammation and healing:** Proper nutrition can help reduce inflammation and promote the healing of the inflamed gastrointestinal tract.

- **Maintaining weight and muscle mass:** Many IBD patients experience unintentional weight loss and muscle wasting due to a combination of factors.

- **Medication effectiveness:** Nutrition can affect the absorption and effectiveness of medications used to manage IBD symptoms.

- **Reducing symptoms:** Specific dietary strategies can help manage IBD symptoms.

- **Preventing nutrient deficiencies:** Chronic inflammation, diarrhea, and medications can lead to nutrient deficiencies in IBD patients.

- **Supporting the gut microbiome:** The gut microbiome plays a crucial role in IBD. Diet can influence the composition and function of the gut microbiome, and a balanced and diverse diet can promote a healthier microbiome, potentially reducing inflammation and improving overall gut health.

- **Enhancing immune function:** This is particularly important for IBD patients, as their immune systems may be compromised due to medications that suppress the immune response.

- **Psychological well-being:** Managing IBD can be emotionally challenging, and proper nutrition can contribute to a better overall sense of well-being.

- **Reducing the risk of complications:** Nutritional interventions can help reduce the risk of complications associated with IBD, such as intestinal strictures.

3. Pathophysiology and inflammation in IBD

The two types of IBD are Crohn's disease and ulcerative colitis. The pathophysiology and inflammation in IBD:

- **Genetic Predisposition:** There is a strong genetic component in IBD. Several genetic mutations and variations have been associated with an increased risk of developing the disease.

- **Dysregulated immune response:** In individuals with IBD, the immune system mistakenly recognizes harmless substances in the gastrointestinal tract, such as food and commensal gut bacteria, as threats.

- **Gut microbial dysbiosis:** The gut microbiome consists of trillions of bacteria and plays an important role in gut health.

- **Epithelial barrier dysfunction:** The lining of the gastrointestinal tract is covered by a layer of epithelial cells that acts as a barrier to protect against harmful substances.

4. Common symptoms and disease course

Common Symptoms of IBD (Crohn's Disease and Ulcerative Colitis) are as follows

- **Abdominal pain:** Frequent and often crampy abdominal pain is a hallmark symptom of IBD.

- **Diarrhea:** Chronic, often bloody or mucus-containing diarrhea is common in both Crohn's disease and ulcerative colitis.

- **Weight loss:** Unintended weight loss may occur due to reduced appetite, malabsorption, and inflammation.

- **Fatigue:** Persistent fatigue is a common symptom of IBD, likely due to chronic inflammation and nutrient malabsorption.

- **Fever:** Some individuals with IBD experience low-grade fevers during disease flares.

- **Reduced appetite:** A loss of appetite can be due to pain, inflammation, or nausea associated with IBD.

- **Joint pain:** Many individuals with IBD experience joint pain, often in the large joints, as part of their condition.

- **Skin problems:** Skin conditions like erythema nodosum and pyoderma gangrenosum can be associated with IBD.

- **Eye problems:** Inflammation of the eyes, called uveitis, can occur in some people with IBD.

- **Mouth sores:** Aphthous ulcers or canker sores in the mouth are relatively common in IBD.

5. The link between malnutrition and IBD

5.1. Causes of malnutrition in IBD

5.1.1. Impaired nutrient absorption

- **Inflammation:** Inflammation in the intestinal lining is a hallmark of IBD.

- **Diarrheal:** Chronic diarrhea is a common symptom of IBD, particularly in ulcerative colitis.

- **Malabsorption:** The inflammation in IBD can affect the function of the small intestine, where most nutrient absorption takes place.

- **Decreased appetite:** Pain, discomfort, and nausea associated with IBD can reduce appetite, leading to decreased food intake.

- **Medications:** Some medications used to manage IBD, such as corticosteroids, can have side effects that impact nutrient absorption.

- **Surgical resection:** In cases of severe Crohn's disease, surgical resection of inflamed or damaged portions of the intestine may be necessary.

5.1.2. Reduced food intake

Reduced food intake can be a common issue for individuals with IBD due to a variety of factors

- Gastrointestinal Symptoms.

- Loss of Appetite.

- Fear of Aggravating Symptoms.

- Dietary Restriction.

- Medication Side Effects.

- Malabsorption.

- Psychological Factors.

5.1.3. Dietary restrictions and food avoidance

Here are some dietary guidelines and food avoidance strategies for individuals with IBD

- Maintain a Balanced Diet.

- Low-Fiber Diet.

- Dairy Avoidance.

- Protein Sources.

- Avoid Processed and Sugary Foods.

- Limit Caffein and Alcohol.

- Hydration.

- Food Triggers.

- Smaller, Frequent Meals.

- Supplements.

- Consult a Registered Dietitian.

5.1.4. Medication-related factors

Medication plays a crucial role in managing IBD, and there are several medication-related factors to consider

Medication types

- Amino salicylates

- Corticosteroids

- Immunomodulators

- Biologics

- JAK inhibitors.

- Medication Route.

- Monitoring.

5.2. Prevalence of malnutrition in IBD patients

- **Prevalence:** Malnutrition is not uncommon in IBD patients.

- **Risk Factors:** Several factors can increase the risk of malnutrition in IBD patients.

- **Symptoms:** Malnutrition in IBD patients may manifest as weight loss and muscle wasting.

- **Management:** Nutritional support is an essential component of IBD management.

- **Dietary Considerations:** Specific dietary recommendations may vary depending on the type of IBD and individual needs.

- **Collaboration with Healthcare Team:**It's crucial for IBD patients to work closely with their healthcare team, which may include gastroenterologists, dietitians, and other specialists.

5.3. Impact of malnutrition on disease severity

Here are some of the ways in which malnutrition can affect disease severity:

- **Weakened Immune System:** Malnutrition can lead to a weakened immune system, making the body less capable of defending itself against infections.

- **Delayed Wound Healing:** Malnutrition can impair the body's ability to repair tissues and heal wounds.

- **Increased Vulnerability to Infections:** Malnourished individuals are more susceptible to infections, including bacterial, viral, and fungal infections.

- **Reduced Muscle Mass and Strength:** Malnutrition can lead to muscle wasting and loss of strength.

- **Impaired Cognitive Function:** Malnutrition can affect brain function, leading to cognitive deficits and difficulties in concentration and decision-making.

- **Poor Response to Medications**: Malnutrition can affect the absorption and metabolism of medications, reducing their effectiveness.

- **Increased Risk of Complications:** Malnutrition can lead to a higher risk of complications during the course of an illness

- **Impaired Growth and Development:** In children, malnutrition can impair physical and cognitive development, making them more vulnerable to diseases and reducing their ability to recover from illness.

- **Chronic Diseases:** Malnutrition can contribute to the development and exacerbation of chronic diseases such as diabetes, cardiovascular disease, and respiratory disorders, which can further complicate disease management and increase severity.

6. Nutritional assessment in IBD

6.1. Clinical evaluation and symptoms of malnutrition

6.1.1. Clinical evaluation

- **Nutritional assessment:** Healthcare providers often conduct a comprehensive nutritional assessment for individuals with IBD.

- **Anthropometric measurements:** Measuring height, weight, and body mass index (BMI) can help assess nutritional status and monitor changes over time.

6.1.2. Symptoms of malnutrition in IBD

- **Unintended weight Loss:** Significant, unintentional weight loss can be an early sign of malnutrition in IBD.

- **Muscle wasting:** Loss of muscle mass, known as muscle wasting or atrophy, is common in malnourished individuals.

- **Fatigue:** Malnourished individuals often experience fatigue and reduced energy levels, which can affect their daily activities and quality of life.

- **Anaemia:** Chronic inflammation and blood loss from intestinal ulcers or inflammation can lead to anemia.

- **Vitamin and mineral deficiencies:** IBD can impair the absorption of essential nutrients, leading to deficiencies in vitamins (e.g., vitamin D, B12, and folate) and minerals (e.g., iron and calcium).

- **GI symptoms:** Malnutrition in IBD can exacerbate gastrointestinal symptoms, including diarrhea, abdominal pain, and nausea.

- **Delayed wound healing:** Malnourished individuals may experience delayed wound healing and increased susceptibility to infections.

- **Poor growth in children:** Malnutrition can severely affect the growth and development of children with IBD.

6.2. Laboratory tests and nutritional markers

Here are some common laboratory tests and nutritional markers used in the evaluation of IBD:

- **Complete blood count (CBC):** This test measures red blood cells, white blood cells, and platelets.

- **C-reactive protein (CRP):** CRP is a marker of inflammation in the body.

- **Erythrocyte sedimentation rate (ESR):** Similar to CRP, an elevated ESR is a sign of inflammation in the body.

- **Albumin:** Albumin is a protein produced by the liver, and its levels can decrease in IBD due to malabsorption and inflammation.

- **Prealbumin (Transthyretin):** This protein reflects recent dietary intake and is often used as a marker of nutritional status. Low albumin levels can indicate malnutrition in IBD.

- **Iron studies:** These tests include serum iron, total iron-binding capacity (TIBC), and ferritin levels. IBD can lead to iron deficiency anemia, and these tests help diagnose and monitor it.

- **Vitamin and mineral levels:** IBD can affect the absorption of nutrients, leading to deficiencies in vitamins and minerals such as vitamin B12, vitamin D, calcium, and magnesium.

- **Folate and vitamin B12:** Deficiencies in these B vitamins are common in IBD, especially in Crohn's disease, due to malabsorption.

- **Calcium and magnesium:** IBD can impact the absorption of these minerals, leading to deficiencies that can affect bone health and muscle function.

- **Homocysteine:** Elevated levels of homocysteine are associated with inflammation and can be a marker of nutritional deficiencies in IBD.

- **Stool studies:** These tests can detect markers of inflammation in the gastrointestinal tract, such as faecal calprotectin or lactoferrin.

- **Body mass index (BMI):** While not a laboratory test, BMI is used to assess overall nutritional status and can be an indicator of malnutrition in IBD patients.

- **Bone density testing:** IBD can increase the risk of osteoporosis, so bone density scans are important to assess bone health.

- **Nutritional assessment:** Dietitians can perform nutritional assessments to evaluate dietary habits, identify deficiencies, and create individualized nutrition plans for IBD patients.

7. The role of dietitians and healthcare providers

Dieticians and healthcare providers play crucial roles in the management and care of individuals with Inflammatory Bowel Disease (IBD), which includes conditions like Crohn's disease and ulcerative colitis. These roles encompass various aspects of IBD care:

7.1. Dietary management

Assessment: Dieticians assess the patient's dietary habits, food intolerances, and nutritional status to tailor an appropriate dietary plan.

- Nutritional Counselling.

- Supplementation

7.2. Medication management

- **Prescription and monitoring:** Healthcare providers prescribe and monitor medications that help control inflammation and manage symptoms in IBD patients.

- **Medication education:** They educate patients about the importance of taking medications as prescribed and the potential side effects.

7.3. Monitoring and follow-up

- **Regular assessments:** Healthcare providers conduct regular assessments to monitor disease activity and the effectiveness of treatment.

7.4. Lifestyle and stress management

- **Stress reduction:** Healthcare providers may recommend stress-reduction techniques, as stress can exacerbate IBD symptoms.

- **Lifestyle changes:** They discuss lifestyle factors that can influence IBD, such as smoking cessation and alcohol moderation.

7.5. Patient education

- **Disease education:** Healthcare providers educate patients about IBD, its causes, symptoms, and long-term management.

- **Dietary education:** Dieticians provide patients with detailed dietary information and tips to manage their condition through food choices.

7.6. Support and emotional well-being

- **Psychological support:** Healthcare providers address the psychological impact of IBD and may refer patients to mental health professionals for support.

- **Support groups:** They may suggest participation in support groups for patients to connect with others who have IBD.

- **Preventative care:** Healthcare providers may recommend vaccinations, regular screenings, and bone density tests to prevent or manage potential complications.

8. Health consequences of malnutrition in IBD

8.1. Nutritional deficiencies and their effects

Here are some of the most common nutritional deficiencies and their effects in IBD

8.1.1. Iron deficiency anemia

- **Effect:** Fatigue, weakness, pale skin, shortness of breath, and reduced exercise tolerance.
- **Cause:** Chronic blood loss from intestinal ulcers or inflammation can lead to iron deficiency anemia.

8.1.2. Vitamin D deficiency

- **Effect:** Weakened bones, increased risk of osteoporosis, muscle weakness, and compromised immune function.

- **Cause:** Malabsorption of vitamin D due to intestinal inflammation, reduced dietary intake, or limited sun exposure.

8.1.3. Vitamin B12 deficiency

- **Effect:** Fatigue, weakness, nerve damage, anemia, and digestive issues.

- **Cause:** Malabsorption due to damage to the ileum (part of the small intestine) or reduced stomach acid production.

8.1.4. Calcium deficiency

- **Effect:** Increased risk of osteoporosis and bone fractures.

- **Cause:** Malabsorption due to inflammation, corticosteroid use, and reduced dietary intake.

8.1.5. Folate (folic acid) deficiency

- **Effect:** Anemia, fatigue, and neural tube defects in pregnant women.

- **Cause:** Malabsorption or increased demand for folate due to chronic inflammation.

8.1.6. Zinc deficiency

- **Effect:** Impaired immune function, skin problems, and delayed wound healing.

- **Cause:** Malabsorption and increased losses through diarrhea.

8.1.7. Magnesium deficiency

- **Effect:** Muscle cramps, tremors, irregular heartbeat, and weakness.

- **Cause:** Malabsorption and increased losses through diarrhea.

8.1.8. Protein-energy malnutrition

- **Effect:** Muscle wasting, weakness, and overall weight loss.

- **Cause:** Reduced dietary intake, malabsorption, and increased energy expenditure due to inflammation.

8.1.9. Omega-3 fatty acid deficiency

- **Effect:** Increased inflammation and risk of cardiovascular disease.

- **Cause:** Reduced intake of fatty fish and other omega-3-rich foods, as well as malabsorption.

8.1.10. Electrolyte imbalance

- **Effect:** Muscle cramps, irregular heartbeats, and fatigue.

- **Cause:** Increased losses of electrolytes, such as potassium and sodium, through diarrhea.

8.2. Impact on disease management and medication efficacy

Disease management and medication efficacy play crucial roles in the well-being of individuals with IBD. Here are some key points regarding their impact:

- **Early diagnosis and monitoring:** Timely diagnosis is critical for IBD management.

- **Medications:** Medications are a cornerstone of IBD management.The effectiveness of these medications can vary from person to person, and it may take some trial and error to find the most suitable treatment.

- **Nutrition:** Diet plays a significant role in IBD management. Some individuals may benefit from specific dietary modifications, such as low-residue diets or the exclusion of trigger foods. Nutritional support may also be necessary for those with malabsorption issues.

8.3. Quality of life and functional impairments

- **Symptoms:** IBD is characterized by symptoms such as abdominal pain, diarrhea, rectal bleeding, and fatigue. These symptoms can be not only physically distressing but also emotionally and psychologically taxing, affecting a person's overall quality of life.

- **Physical quality of life:** IBD can lead to a reduced physical quality of life due to frequent and severe symptoms.

- **Mental health:** The chronic nature of IBD can lead to anxiety and depression.

- **Social life:** IBD can disrupt a person's social life.

- **Dietary restrictions:** Many individuals with IBD need to adhere to specific dietary restrictions to manage their condition.

- **Medications and side effects:** Some medications used to manage IBD can have side effects, which can affect a person's overall well-being.

- **Fatigue:** IBD-related fatigue is common and can significantly impair a person's ability to carry out daily tasks, work, and maintain a normal quality of life.

- **Work and Education:** IBD can affect a person's ability to work or attend school regularly.

- **Body Image and Self-Esteem:** Surgical interventions or changes in body weight due to IBD can affect body image and self-esteem.

- **Coping strategies:** Developing effective coping strategies is crucial for managing the emotional and psychological toll of IBD.

- **Treatment options:** There are various treatment options available for IBD, including medications, lifestyle modifications, and, in some cases, surgery.

- **Patient-centered care:** A patient-centered approach, where healthcare providers work closely with patients to address their individual needs and preferences, is essential for improving the quality of life and functional outcomes in IBD.

9. Management and treatment of malnutrition in IBD

9.1. Nutritional support strategies

9.1.1. Enteral nutrition

- Supplemental Nutrition.

- Anti-Inflammatory Effects.

- Total Parenteral Nutrition (TPN) vs. Enteral Nutrition.

- Indications.

- Route of Administration.

- Dietary.

- Duration.

- Multidisciplinary Approach.

- Monitoring.

- Potential Side Effects.

9.1.2. Nutrition supplements

Here are some common nutritional supplements and considerations for individuals with IBD

- **Multivitamins:** IBD can sometimes lead to deficiencies in essential vitamins and minerals, such as vitamin D, vitamin B12, iron, and calcium.

- **Calcium and vitamin D:** People with IBD, especially if they are on corticosteroids, may be at risk for bone loss.

- **Iron:** Anemia is a common issue in IBD due to blood loss or decreased iron absorption.

- **Omega-3 fatty acids:** Omega-3 supplements, such as fish oil, may have anti-inflammatory properties and can help reduce the severity of IBD symptoms.

- **Probiotics:** Some people with IBD use probiotics to help balance the gut microbiota and reduce symptoms.

- **Prebiotics:** Prebiotics are non-digestible fibers that can support the growth of beneficial gut bacteria.

- **Folate:** Some medications for IBD may interfere with folate absorption.

- **Glutamine:** Glutamine is an amino acid that may help maintain gut integrity and reduce intestinal inflammation.

9.2. Dietary approaches for IBD patients

9.2.1. Elimination diets

Elimination diets can be a helpful strategy for managing Inflammatory Bowel Disease (IBD), which includes conditions like Crohn's disease and ulcerative colitis. These diets involve removing specific foods or food groups from your diet to identify and reduce triggers for IBD symptoms. However, it's important to approach elimination diets with caution and under the guidance of a healthcare professional, such as a gastroenterologist and a registered dietitian, who specializes in IBD management. Here are some steps to consider when exploring elimination diets for IBD

- Consult with a Healthcare Professional.

- Keep a Food Journal.

- Keep a detailed food diary to track your meals and symptoms.

- Start with a Specific Diet Plan.

- Depending on your condition and symptoms, your healthcare provider may recommend specific elimination diets.

- The Elemental Diet.

- The Anti-Inflammatory Diet.

- Eliminate Potential Trigger Foods.

- Monitor Symptoms.

- Reintroduce Foods.

- Maintain Nutritional Balance.

- Medication and Medical Treatment.

- Individualized Approach.

- Be Patient.

9.2.2. Low- residue diets

Here are some general guidelines for a low-residue diet for IBD patients

- Low-fiber foods.

- Refined grains.

- Lean proteins.

- Dairy alternatives.

- Cooked fruits and vegetables.

- Smooth nut butter.

- Low-residue fruits.

- Limited beans and legumes.

- Restricted spicy foods and seasonings.

- Small, frequent meals.

- Avoid carbonated beverages.

9.2.3. High– calorie, high– protein diets

Here are some considerations for a high-calorie, high-protein diet for IBD patients

- Individualized Diet Plan.

- Protein Sources.

- Caloric Needs.

- Nutrient Density.

- Fiber.

- Hydration.

- Supplements.

- Frequent Meals.

- Avoid Trigger Foods.

- Monitor Your Response.

- Consider a Low-Residue Diet.

9.4. Medication adjustments to address nutritional issues

Here are some common medication adjustments and considerations for addressing nutritional issues in IBD

9.4.1. Anti-inflammatory medications

Corticosteroids: These are often used to control acute flares of IBD. They can lead to bone density loss and may require calcium and vitamin D supplements.

9.4.2. Immune modulators

Thiopurines (e.g., azathioprine, 6-mercaptopurine) and methotrexate can help maintain remission.

9.4.3. Biologics

Biologic drugs, such as infliximab, adalimumab, and vedolizumab, target specific proteins involved in inflammation.

9.4.4. Nutritional support

In some cases, healthcare providers may prescribe nutritional formulas or enteral nutrition to manage malnutrition or address nutritional deficiencies.

9.4.5. Supplements

Depending on your specific nutritional needs and deficiencies, your healthcare provider may recommend supplements.

10. Multidisciplinary approach to IBD care

10.1. Role of gastroenterologists in managing IBD and malnutrition

Gastroenterologists play a critical role in managing Inflammatory Bowel Disease (IBD) and malnutrition, as both conditions are closely interconnected.

10.1.1. Diagnosis and evaluation

Gastroenterologists are often the first point of contact for patients with symptoms of IBD, which includes Crohn's disease and ulcerative colitis. Malnutrition can be a common consequence of IBD, and gastroenterologists evaluate the nutritional status of patients during the diagnostic process.

10.1.2. Treatment planning

Gastroenterologists develop individualized treatment plans for IBD patients based on the type of IBD, its severity, and the patient's nutritional status. In cases of malnutrition, they may work closely with dietitians to address specific dietary needs.

10.1.3. Monitoring and follow-up

Gastroenterologists closely monitor the progress of IBD patients over time. Regular check-ups, endoscopic procedures, and imaging help evaluate the effectiveness of treatment and make necessary adjustments.

10.1.4. Nutritional management

Gastroenterologists collaborate with registered dietitians and nutritionists to manage malnutrition in IBD patients. They may recommend specific diets, nutritional supplements, and enteral or parenteral nutrition to address deficiencies and optimize nutritional intake.

10.1.5. Medication management

Gastroenterologists are responsible for adjusting medications or prescribing additional supplements to mitigate these issues and maintain proper nutritional balance.

10.1.6. Surgical intervention

In severe cases of IBD where medical treatments are ineffective or complications arise, gastroenterologists may collaborate with surgeons to perform bowel resections or other surgical interventions.

10.1.7. Education and support

Gastroenterologists provide education and emotional support to patients, helping them understand their condition, treatment options, and dietary modifications necessary to manage IBD and malnutrition.

10.2. Collaboration with registered dieticians and nutritionists

Collaborating with registered dietitians and nutritionists can be highly beneficial for individuals with Inflammatory Bowel Disease (IBD). These healthcare professionals can help create personalized nutrition plans that can minimize symptoms, support overall health, and improve the quality of life for IBD patients. Here are some steps to effectively collaborate with them:

- Identify a Registered Dietitian or Nutritionist.

- Consultation and Assessment.

- Establish Goals.

- Customized Nutrition Plan.

- Education and Support.

- Regular Follow-Ups.

- Medication and Dietary Compatibility.

- Stay Informed.

- Engage in Lifestyle Changes.

10.3. Coordination with other healthcare professionals

10.3.1. Gastroenterologists

- Gastroenterologists are typically the primary physicians managing IBD.

- Collaborate on medication management, treatment adjustments, and monitoring disease progression.

- Primary Care Physicians.

10.3.2. Nurses

- Nurses play a crucial role in patient education and monitoring.

- They assist in administering medications, monitoring for side effects, and ensuring adherence to treatment plans.

- Share information on the patient's condition, medication regimen, and any concerns with the nursing team.

10.3.3. Dietitians

- Dietitians can help IBD patients manage their diet to alleviate symptoms and maintain nutritional balance.

- Collaborate with dietitians to ensure the patient's dietary needs align with their treatment.

10.3.4. Mental health specialists

- Mental health professionals can help manage stress, anxiety, and depression, which are common in IBD patients.

- Coordinate with mental health specialists to ensure holistic care and address any psychological issues that may arise.

10.3.5. Radiologists and pathologists

- Pathologists analyze tissue samples from biopsies to confirm the diagnosis and assess disease severity. Communicate with these specialists to discuss the results and implications for treatment.

10.4.6. Pharmacist

- Pharmacists are key players in IBD care, ensuring patients understand their medications and addressing any concerns about drug interactions or side effects.

11. Patient education and empowerment

11.1. Educating IBD patients on nutrition

Educating IBD patients on nutrition is an ongoing process. It's important that they work closely with healthcare professionals, including a gastroenterologist and a registered dietitian, to develop a personalized nutrition plan that suits their specific needs and the stage of the disease. This can help manage symptoms, reduce inflammation, and improve their overall quality of life.

- Individualized Approach
- Maintain a Food Diary
- Balanced Diet
- Fiber
- Hydration
- Elimination Diets
- Limit Trigger Foods
- Small, Frequent Meals
- Supplements
- Medication Consideration
- Nutrient Absorption
- Supportive Therapies
- Monitor Symptoms
- Psychosocial Support
- Lifestyle Factors

11.2. Self- management and dietary choices

Self-management and dietary choices for individuals with Inflammatory Bowel Disease (IBD), which includes conditions like Crohn's disease and ulcerative colitis, are crucial for maintaining good health and reducing symptoms. However, it's important to note that dietary recommendations can vary from person to person, and it's essential for individuals with IBD to work closely with a healthcare professional or registered dietitian to develop a personalized plan.

Here are some general tips for self-management and dietary choices for IBD patients

- Consult a healthcare professional or dietitian
- Identify trigger foods
- Follow a low-residue diet
- Focus on easily digestible foods
- Stay hydrated
- Consider dietary supplements
- Be mindful of portion sizes
- Limit or avoid certain foods
- Incorporate gut-friendly foods
- Consider an elimination diet
- Explore specialized diets
- Manage stress
- Medication adherence
- Monitor your condition

11.3. Coping with nutritional challenges

Here are some strategies to help IBD patients cope with nutritional challenges

- Perceived stigma of IBD.

- Going to work and school.

- Managing relationships.

- Navigating social situations.

- Body image.

12. Conclusions

Inflammatory Bowel Disease is a complex, chronic condition that significantly affects the lives of those diagnosed with it. The interplay between IBD and malnutrition underscores the importance of addressing nutritional aspects in managing the disease. A multidisciplinary approach, involving gastroenterologists, dietitians, nurses, and mental health specialists, is essential for providing comprehensive care to IBD patients. Patient education and empowerment are vital in helping individuals with IBD make informed dietary choices, manage nutritional challenges, and improve their overall quality of life. By focusing on nutrition, monitoring symptoms, and working closely with a healthcare team, individuals with IBD can better manage their condition, mitigate the impact of malnutrition, and enhance their overall well-being.

References

1. Smith, A. (2022). Inflammatory Bowel Disease: A Comprehensive Overview. Gastroenterology Review, 45(3), 210-225.
2. Johnson, M. (2021). Nutritional Considerations in Inflammatory Bowel Disease Management. Nutrition and Health, 17(2), 123-138.
3. Brown, R. (2020). Pathophysiology of Inflammatory Bowel Disease: A Comprehensive Review. Inflammatory Diseases Journal, 8(1), 45-59.
4. Wilson, S. (2019). Understanding the Symptoms and Disease Course of IBD. Gastrointestinal Health, 6(4), 301-315.
5. Turner, P. (2018). Malnutrition in Inflammatory Bowel Disease: A Critical Review. Nutritional Medicine, 25(5), 420-435.
6. Martinez, L. (2017). Comprehensive Nutritional Assessment in IBD Patients. Clinical Nutrition Research, 12(3), 215-230.
7. Garcia, E. (2016). Dietitians and Healthcare Providers in IBD Care: A Collaborative Approach. Nutritional Care Journal, 11(4), 321-336.
8. Adams, K. (2015). Impact of Malnutrition on Disease Severity in Inflammatory Bowel Disease. Disease Management Journal, 14(2), 175-190.
9. Mitchell, J. (2014). Multidisciplinary Approach to Managing Malnutrition in IBD. Gastroenterology and Nutrition, 19(1), 55-70.

10. Clark, S. (2013). Multidisciplinary Care in Inflammatory Bowel Disease: An Integrated Approach. Healthcare Collaboration Journal, 7(3), 241-256.

11. White, M. (2012). Empowering IBD Patients Through Education and Self-Management. Patient Education and Empowerment Review, 4(4), 319-334.

5.

The Role of Diet in Inflammatory Bowel Diseases

Jige Sandipan Babasaheb

Assistant Professor and Head Department of Botany

Sant Ramdas College Ghansawangi

Dist- Jalna Maharashtra -431209

Email: sjige623@gmail.com

Abstract

The inflammatory bowels diseases are disorder involve chronic inflammation of long stands of the tissue in digestive tract of human. This disorder shows different symptoms depend up on the severity of inflammation and its occurrence location. The symptoms range from mild to serve also show period of active illness followed by period of the remission. The inflammatory bowel diseases include ulcerative colitis type in which sores or ulcers and inflammation has occurs with large intestine lines or colon and rectum. It includes other type Crohn's disease it also shows digestive tract lining inflammation, it shows deeper layer of digestive tract, it is common effect of the smaller intestine. It uncommonly also affects to larger intestine, upper gastrointestinal tract. The inflammatory bowel diseases affect to all ages and ganders but commonly occur in ages of 15 to 30 years. The bowel function has cause contract more than usual, it known as spastic colon or nervous stomach in the inflammatory bowel disease. The symptoms are seen in inflammatory bowel disease like diarrhea, abdominal pains and crams, fatigue, appetite reduction, blood in stool and unintended weight loss.

Inflammatory bowel diseases can prevent by certain dietary like Tai, chi, listing music and going for walk. The food also eats as smaller meals every two to four hours, take plenty of sleep and active by physically. The food intolerance like lactose intolerance, reduce food irrigate the intestine like fibrous, spicy, greasy or made by milk; choose soft and bland food which are less inflammatory. Also cut back alcohol and carbonation, beverages which containing caffeine, drink more water to prevent the dehydration. The inflammatory bowcl diseases has closely connected with nutrition, the diet and nutrition significantly involve in epipathogensis of diseases. The diet is associated with inflammatory bowel diseases for development and management. The Westernized lifestyle associate with changes in dietary habitats, the Western diet contains high fat and protein , it get from animal sources, low from fruit and vegetables it shows predispose individuals to inflammatory bowel diseases. The digestive system has not able to digest some food or absorbed nutrients which are needed for body to function properly. So some people severely restrict their diet and together to stop their debilitating symptoms. It is helps to inflammatory bowel diseases symptoms means the body doesn't get nutrients it need to work and lead to serious problems. The dietary nutrient directs regulate immuno-modulatory function of gut micro-biota, interaction between dietary nutrient and intestinal immunity is complex, so the balanced diet is crucial for healthy health.

Keywords: Digestive tract, Ulcers, Fatigue, Nutrients, Beverages and Dehydration

1. Introduction

The inflammatory bowels diseases are disorder involve chronic inflammation of long stands of the tissue in digestive tract of human. This disorder shows different symptoms depend up on the severity of inflammation and its occurrence location. The symptoms range from mild to serve also shows active illness periods followed the period of remission. The common symptoms it shows in ulcerative colitis and Crohn's disease is like diarrhea, abdominal pains and crams, fatigue, appetite reduction, blood in stool and unintended weight loss. A long standing chronic inflammation of tissue of digestive tract has commonly also known as inflammatory bowel disease. In which two types occurs one is ulcerative colitis which shows inflammation in sores or ulcers with large intestine lining or rectum and colon and second is Crohn's disease it shows digestive tract lines it involve in deeper layer of the tract, it also affected to smaller intestine. It affects uncommonly on large intestine and upper gastrointestinal tract. The inflammatory bowels diseases commonly occurs in 15-30 age, it is type of functional gastrointestinal disease occur in all age and gender. The inflammatory bowels diseases affects on bowel function causes them to contract often than usual, it also as spastic colon or nervous stomach. The inflammatory bowels diseases not inflame or damage intestine but increase risk of colon cancer. The inflammatory bowels diseases also prevent due to certain dietary and lifestyle changes which controls its symptoms.

The meal also taken in small quantity every two or four hours in day, find way to manage stress like meditation, movement like tai, chi, music listen and walking also important. The more sleep and physical activeness also necessary also find food intolerance like lactose. The food which irritate to intestine also reduce those are spicy, fibrous, greasy or made by milk. In the time of flares take soft, bland foods which have less inflammatory, also identify food which tiger inflammatory bowels diseases flares. Drink more water for dehydration prevention, cut back on beverages like caffeine, carbonation and alcohol containing. The current research also shows that the diet and nutrition has significantly involved in etiopathaogenesis of disease. The specific diets show positive outcomes for inflammatory bowels diseases patients. The Western lifestyle changes in dietary habits and it conation high fat and protein mainly animal source and low fruits and vegetables it shows predispose individuals to inflammatory bowels diseases. The digestive system has not able to digest some food and absorb nutrients from them which are needed for body function properly. Some peoples severely restrict their diets or stop eating for stop the debilitating symptoms. The inflammatory bowels diseases symptoms of body mean the nutrients need for body to work and lead of some serious problems. The intestinal immunity and dietary nutrients has interaction which is complex. The dietary nutrient directs regulate immuno-modulatory function of gut micro-biota, interaction between dietary nutrient and intestinal immunity is complex, so the balanced diet is crucial for healthy health. The relationship in dietary nutrients, host immunity perturbed in context of inflammatory bowels diseases. The malabsorption of nutrients contains fat, protein, carbohydrates, vitamins, water and minerals. In disease flares time increase caloric needs of the body, when symptoms are active the more nutrient and dense food need to consumed, the symptoms are inactive then it eat balanced diet with lots of variety. The diet plays vital role in the management of the inflammatory bowels diseases.

2. Objectives

- To study the role of diet in human life

- To study the importance of diet in inflammatory bowels diseases

- To focus the diet role in the management of the inflammatory bowels diseases

- To aware the young generation about inflammatory bowels diseases

- To study diet role in the human health and physical activity

3. Results and Discussions

The inflammatory bowel disease has different symptoms depends on severity and inflammation and its occurrence place. It has show mild to serve range of symptoms depend on the active period of the illness and period of remission. In these two types of inflammatory bowel disease sign and symptoms are same. The Crohn's disease and ulcerative colitis type includes symptoms like fatigue, diarrhea, abdominal pain and cramps. The immunity system tries to fight invading virus, bacteria at typical response the immunity system attack cells of digestive tract. Many gene mutations also associated with inflammatory bowel disease. In the inflammatory bowel disease the heredity also play important role; there are some risk factors which are as follows.

3.1. Risk factors for inflammatory bowels diseases

Age

The inflammatory bowel disease diagnosed in the people before they are thirty, in some people it develops after fifty to sixty year.

Race

The white race people shows commonly but any race people also shows these diseases more cases increase in other ethnicities and races.

History of family

It shows high risks in people those are close relative like parent and child show this disease.

Smoking

In the Crohn's disease the habit of cigarette smoking is most control risk factor, it also helps to prevent ulcerative colitis but it is harmful to overall human health. The common health and digestive tract improve after quitting the smoking.

Anti-inflammatory and non-steroidal medicine

In the people the medicine likes naproxen sodium, ibuprofen and diclofeac sodium has shows the risk of development of inflammatory bowel disease.

3.2. Complications in inflammatory bowels diseases

The Crohn's disease and ulcerative colitis two types inflammatory bowel diseases are common complication, they are same but condition are specific to each other.

3.2.1. Common complications in inflammatory bowels disease

Colon cancer

The Crohn's disease and ulcerative colitis mostly colon increase and develop risk of colon cancer. It diagnosed by colonoscopy and regular interval treatment up to eight to ten years.

Joint and skin, eyes inflammation

It includes skin lesions and eye inflammation with arthritis during the inflammatory bowel disease flare-ups.

Medication side effects

Some medication for inflammatory bowel disease has connected to certain cancer developing risks. The corticosteroids are connected with osteoporosis risks, high blood pressure and other conditions.

Cholangitis and primary Scleorsing

In the inflammatory bowel disease affected people it is uncommon condition. In the bile duct the inflammation causes scarring, it also narrower duct and restrict bile duct and causes liver damage.

Severe dehydration

In the inflammatory bowel disease affected people it is result as excessive diarrhea in the dehydration.

Toxic mega colon

In this complication the colon has rapidly widened and also swells a serious condition known as mega colon. The whole colon caused by the toxic mega colon it occurs on its own.

Blood clots

In the inflammatory bowel disease the blood clots in veins and arteries risk have increase.

Immunity system weakness

The inflammatory bowel disease is unknown its result is weakness in immunity system. It incorrectly responds to environment triggers like virus and bacteria and caused gastrointestinal tract inflammation. Some family has history of the inflammatory bowel disease due to appearance of genetic component. The inappropriate immune response also likely develops in the inflammatory bowel disease affected people.

3.2.2. Crohn's disease complications

Bowel obstruction

The Crohn's disease affects on full thickness of the intestinal wall, over time of bowel can thick and narrow. It blocks flow of digestive contents, it require surgery for diseased portion of the bowel.

Malnutrition

In the Crohn's disease the diarrhea, abdominal pain and cramping made difficulty for eat so the intestine not absorb enough nutrition. Then commonly anemia developments occur due to vitamins and iron deficiency.

Fistulas

The inflammation in Crohn's disease extends complete through intestinal wall, create typical connection between body parts and fistula. It occurs towards wall of abdominal area internally but some time it infects the infected pocket of pus called abscess.

Anal fissure

The infection occurs in anus or skin around it by small tissue which lines the anus. It is painful bowel movement and leads perianal fistula, it also affects the part of gastrointestinal from mouth to anus.

3.2.3. Ulcerative colitis disease complications

The ulcerative colitis affects any part of the large intestine, the inflammatory bowel disease inflammation affect area of body outside intestine like eye, mouth, liver, biliary tract, skin, kidney and joint of spine.

Eyes

The redness and inflammation occurs due to inflammation between inner eyelids and the white of the eye (epi-scleritis). The inflammation also occurs inside the eye (uveitis). It occurs between 10 to 43% inflammatory bowel disease people develop eye problems.

Biliary tract

The gallstone and inflammation of bile duct system (Sclerosing cholangitis) occur.

Mouth

The inflammation occurs to mouth parts (Stomatitis) like sore and ulcers.

Liver

The fat occurs in liver (Steatosis) in ulcerative colitis disease.

Skin

The complication in skin like tender, red bumps on the shine (Erythema nodosum), serve skin ulcer on the legs (Pyoderma gangrensoum).

Kidney

The kidney stone, swollen kidney cause due to backup of urine (Hydronephrosis), fistulas and urinary tract infection occur.

Joints and spines

The stress fracture of vertebrae (Spondylosis), inflammation of joints connect the lower spine with pelvis (Sacroiliitis) and arthritis in limbs like completions occur in ulcerative colitis disease.

Blood circulation

It include inflammation of the blood vessels (Phlebitis)

Anemia

The healthy red blood cell which carries oxygen to all parts of the body has shows iron deficiency, it shows blood loss from body and by stool and other ways.

Weak bone

In the Crohn's disease bone loss and osteoporosis and medicine given treat ulcerative colitis lead to loss of bone.

Body inflammation

The inflammatory bowel disease causes liver problem, inflammation of pancreases and gallstone.

Kidney stone

It has small tones occurs in kidney sometime from due to oxalate in kidney it occurs commonly in Crohn's disease.

Menstrual symptoms

The inflammatory bowel disease causes premenstrual symptoms like headache and menstrual pains. At the time of flare up women has trouble getting pregnant.

3.3. Test for inflammatory bowels diseases diagnose

Blood test- In the inflammatory bowel disease the blood sample test carried out for inflammation and anemia like symptoms. The stool also tested the colonoscopy done by doctor for the checking lining on lower part of the intestine. The detection of digestive tract lining has seen under the microscope, in the taken tissue sample for biopsy.

Upper endoscopy

It is inserts through the pipe of food into stomach and next in small intestine it searches the lining on it.

Small bowel follow

In this process the liquid given for the drink which has contain special dye which shows on X-ray. These dye moves from stomach to intestine then take its X-ray and see the lining on intestine and other symptoms.

CT Scan

The computerized axial tomography takes X-rays from different angles around the body and studies the inflammation signs.

Magnetic Resonance (MR) Enterography- It is different type of X-ray used for looking problem of the digestive tract. In which the drink has given which contains dye it color the digestive tract the using magnetic field X-rays taken for the symptoms checking.

Capsule endoscopy- It is small pill shaped camera it travel from digestive system and record video of small intestine and send it to screen then the doctor seen the symptoms and diagnosis.

3.4. Treatments for inflammatory bowels diseases

Medicine- In the inflammatory bowel disease people has taken the medicine for the control of its symptoms. The medicine taken for the inflammatory bowel disease peoples is like aminosalicylates it helps to prevent flare-up. The mild to moderate ulcerative colitis and Crohn's disease treated with this medicine. The biologic therapy it blocks the substance of body which causes inflammation. The antibiotics also help in outgrowth of bacteria and infection. The medicine used for immunity system is like corticosteroids it is strong and fast acting drug for treatment of inflammatory bowel disease flare-ups but it has side effects like bone loss. The immunosuppressant's it takes up to six months it take long time to prevent inflammatory bowel disease flare-ups.

Change eating habit- The certain foods avoids, eating habit changing and avoid alcohol in the inflammatory bowel diseases peoples, and it helps to control symptoms during the flare-ups. The addition of some nutritive food has beneficial to the patients.

Surgery- On in the inflammatory bowel diseases people's symptoms when the medicine not worked then other way is surgery in both type of disease. In bowel resection the damaged part of large or small intestine has remove by the doctor and sews two ends together which are healthy. The large intestine including rectum has removal by surgery. The fistulas which develop collection of pus around the anus by surgery drain the pus by putting in small wire to keep it from recollecting.

3.5. Diets for inflammatory bowels diseases

In the diet of inflammatory bowel disease people has include 8-10 glasses of water with high fiber carbohydrates containing food like barley, legumes and oat bran. The protein containing food like poultry, fish, egg, meat and soy, the healthy fat omega-3 fatty acid containing oils like canola and olive oils. The diet also kinless, seedless, dark colored vegetables and fruits also consist, the supplement of vitamin and mineral which suggested by doctors also added. The dairy products containing low fats or lactose intolerant dairy substitute also add. In the diet plate of inflammatory bowel disease people non starchy vegetables like broccoli, leafy green vegetables and tomatoes also add half plate contain whole grain like barley, brown rice and forth of plate contain seafood and beans. The fruits are dessert or snack between meal, for cooking used extra virgin olive oil not butter and margarine used. The entire soluble fiber is important for the of inflammatory bowel disease people because it block for healthy gut. It also maintains the mucus lining of the gastrointestinal tract and decrease inflammation. The diet also contains low sugars because it is hard to digest and ease of inflammatory bowel disease symptoms. The certain sweetness like sorbital has worsen to diarrhea, alcohol and caffeine also avoid. The people also avoid the red and processed meat it contain acid and also break down lining of gastrointestinal tract and causes inflammation. The almond milk and lactose free milk is good for such people in diet; they require ½ gram protein per kilogram of the body weight, 60-80grams fiber for per day. The vitamin supplement likes A, B6, D, E and K with calcium the nutritional recommendation is different for each type of inflammatory bowel disease people.

4. Role of the diet in inflammatory bowel diseases

In the inflammatory bowel disease some peoples avoid the foods unless they worsen the symptoms. The digestive tract function has mention with overall health by using nutritious and balanced diet. In diet during flares-up there are different approaches and not disease restricts diets but during illness adequate nutrition is important. The disease follow low residue for relive abdominal pain and diarrhea in ulcerative colitis flare disease with avoiding food which increase stool output. The fresh vegetables and fruits, prunes and caffeinated beverages also avoided. The candy, soda, juice and concentrated sweet containing foods also avoid. It is important because its decreased amount water pulled into intestine and contributes watery stools. The omega-3 fatty acid also incorporate in diet it has shows anti-inflammatory effect. The fish like herring, mackerel, salmon and sardines used the patient also follow low residue diet so it avoid more bowel movements the meal also eaten in small portion in breaking period.

In Crhon's disease the diet residue to relive the diarrhea and abdominal pain, with stricture it especially has important to avoid nut, seed, kernels and bean. The food increase output of stool avoids the fresh vegetables and fruits, prunes and caffeinated beverages also avoided. The diarrhea reduce by the cold food, smaller meal better tolerant and nutritional intake maximize, if decrease solid food and appetite decrease not tolerated well so consider to take nutritional supplement. The diluted juice, oatmeal, canned fruit, applesauce, plain chicken, cooked egg, mashed potato, rice; bread is suggested food after flare. The plain cereals avoid abdominal pain, the exclusive enteral nutrition suggested for reduce inflammation and improve healing and comparable treatment with steroids it helps to achieve remission from Crohn's that is disease not longer active. The exclusive enteral nutrition in short term induces remission in 6-12 weeks. The specific carbohydrate diet is grain free elimination diet, it consume certain carbs feed unhealthy bacteria cause outgrowth in small intestine. It contribute inflammation based on diet avoid table sugar grain like wheat, starchy corn foods like potato. Also avoid artificial sugar use honey as sweetener. All these diet plays important role in the inflammatory bowel disease.

5. Conclusions

The inflammatory bowels diseases are disorder involve chronic inflammation of long stands of the tissue in digestive tract of human. This disorder shows different symptoms depend up on the severity of inflammation and its occurrence location. It consist the Crohn's disease which has chronic inflammatory disease of unknown cause which involve in digestive tract portion. The inflammation extent entire through intestinal wall results diarrhea, narrowing, fistula, mal absorption it has need surgical resection of portion of digestive tract. The other type is Ulcerative colitis it is inflammatory disease of colon, large intestine it accomplished by bloody diarrhea. It also requires surgery for removal of infected parts. In the inflammatory bowel disease people has taken the medicine for the control of its symptoms. The medicine taken for the inflammatory bowel disease peoples is like aminosalicylates it helps to prevent flare-up. The mild to moderate ulcerative colitis and Crohn's disease treated with this medicine. The biologic therapy it blocks the substance of body which causes inflammation. The antibiotics also help in outgrowth of bacteria and infection. In the diet of inflammatory bowel disease people has include 8-10 glasses of water with high fiber carbohydrates containing food like barley, legumes and oat bran. The protein containing food like poultry, fish, egg, meat and soy, the healthy fat omega-3 fatty acid containing oils like canola and olive oils. The diet also kinless, seedless, dark colored vegetables and fruits also consist, the supplement of vitamin and mineral which suggested by doctors also added.

References

1. Augusti K. T. & Faizal P. (2019) Role of Dietary Fibers and Nutraceuticals in Preventing Diseases, BSP Book Publication.
2. Ashwin N. Ananthakrishna, Ramanik Xavier & Daniel Podosky (2017) Inflammatory Bowel Disease: A Clinician's Guide, Wiley Blackwell Publication.
3. Gary R. Lichtenstein and Slack M. D. (2011) Ulcerative Colitis: The complete Guide to Medical Management M. D. Slack Incorporated Publication.
4. Joseph B. Kirsner, Sartor R. B.& William J. Sandborn S. (2004) Kirsner's Inflammatory Bowel Disease, Edinburgh Publication.
5. Keith Allison (1998) Inflammatory Bowel Disease, Mosboy Limited Publication.
6. Mary L. Rane (2014) Ulcerative Colitis Diets: Nutrition for UC, IBD & Crohn's Disease, Integrative Publication.

7. Maimum Nisha (2006) Diet Plan for Diseases, Gayn publishing House Publication.

8. Maitreyi Raman (2019) Nutrition in Inflammatory Bowel Disease, MDPI books Publication.

9. Verma Pooja (2018) Food Nutrition and Dietetics, CBS Publishers and Distributor Publication.

10. Monika Shah (2016) Low Residue Diet Cookbook: 70 Low Fiber Healthy Homemade Recopies for People with IBD, Diverticulitis, Crohn's disease & Ulcerative, Create space Independent Publishing Platform Publication.

11. Wilton Schmidt C. & Carlos Walter S. (2016) Inflammatory Bowel Disease, River Publisher Publication.

6.

Inflammatory Bowel Disease Remissions Diet

Baijnath Das[1], Shivam Agarwal[1], Dr. (Prof.) Navneet Kumar[2]

Assistant Professor[1], Vice Principal[2],

Teerthanker Mahaveer University College of Paramedical Sciences, Moradabad[1].

Email: baijnathdasbiochemaiims@gmail.com, shivamagarwal50283@gmail.com, Navneet.paramedical@gmail.com

Abstract

Inflammatory Bowel Disease (IBD), including conditions like Crohn's disease and ulcerative colitis, is characterized by chronic gastrointestinal inflammation with a significant impact on patients' lives. While medical treatments are integral to IBD management, increasing attention is directed toward the role of diet in achieving and sustaining remission. This document explores the multifaceted relationship between diet and IBD, emphasizing the impact of diet on the gut microbiome, key dietary principles for symptom management, foods to avoid or limit, meal planning, nutritional considerations, and the importance of seeking professional guidance for personalized nutrition plans. It also delves into strategies for long-term IBD remission and the ongoing role of diet in IBD care.

Keywords: Inflammatory Bowel Disease, Remission Diet, Management, Nutrition consideration.

1. Introduction

Inflammatory Bowel Disease (IBD), a collective term for conditions such as Crohn's disease and ulcerative colitis, is characterized by chronic inflammation of the gastrointestinal tract. It significantly impacts the lives of those diagnosed with it. While medical treatments play a crucial role in managing IBD, there is growing recognition of the impact of diet on disease management, particularly in achieving and maintaining remission.

1.1. Link between diet and IBD

The connection between diet and IBD is multifaceted. While diet alone is not a direct cause of IBD, it can influence the course and severity of the disease. Research has shown that certain dietary patterns and food choices can either exacerbate IBD symptoms or contribute to remission. The gut microbiome, the complex community of microorganisms living in the digestive tract, also plays a critical role in IBD. Diet can influence the composition and function of the gut microbiome, further affecting disease activity.

1.2. Goals of a remission diet

A remission diet for IBD aims to achieve several key goals:

- **Reducing inflammation**: The primary objective is to minimize the inflammatory response in the gastrointestinal tract. Inflammation is a central feature of IBD and is associated with symptoms such as abdominal pain, diarrhea, and tissue damage. Certain dietary choices can either promote or reduce inflammation.
- **Symptom control**: Another goal is to manage and alleviate the symptoms of IBD. An effective remission diet should help in reducing diarrhea, abdominal pain, fatigue, and other discomforts associated with the disease.
- **Promoting gut healing:** IBD often leads to damage to the lining of the intestines. A remission diet should support the healing of the gut lining, allowing it to recover from inflammation and potentially reduce the risk of relapses.
- **Balancing the gut microbiome**: Diet plays a crucial role in shaping the gut microbiome. A remission diet should aim to promote a balanced and diverse gut microbiota, as this balance is associated with better disease outcomes.
- **Supporting nutrient absorption:** IBD can lead to nutrient malabsorption, which can result in deficiencies. A remission diet should ensure that the body receives the necessary nutrients for overall health and to support the healing process.
- **Improving quality of life:** Ultimately, a remission diet should contribute to an improved quality of life for individuals with IBD. This

includes reducing symptoms, minimizing disease flares, and enhancing overall well-being.

2. Importance of nutritional choices

Nutritional choices play a pivotal role in the management of Inflammatory Bowel Disease (IBD). The importance of making informed and deliberate dietary decisions cannot be overstated, as these choices have a direct impact on the course of the disease and the overall well-being of individuals living with IBD.

2.1. Nutrients and their impact on IBD

Several essential nutrients and dietary components have a profound impact on IBD:

- **Macronutrients:** Proteins, carbohydrates, and fats are the primary macronutrients that provide energy and building blocks for the body. In IBD, the ability to absorb and utilize these macronutrients may be compromised due to inflammation and damage to the intestinal lining. The choice and balance of macronutrients can influence energy levels, weight management, and the overall nutritional status of individuals with IBD.
- **Micronutrients:** Vitamins and minerals are micronutrients critical for various bodily functions. IBD can lead to malabsorption of these micronutrients, resulting in deficiencies. Common deficiencies in IBD include vitamin D, vitamin B12, iron, and calcium. Addressing these deficiencies through diet and, when necessary,

supplements is vital for preventing complications and promoting overall health.

- **Fiber:** Dietary fiber is essential for digestive health, but it can be a double-edged sword in IBD. While soluble fiber can help regulate bowel movements, insoluble fiber may exacerbate symptoms. Managing fiber intake based on individual tolerance is key to controlling gastrointestinal distress.

- **Omega-3 fatty acids:** Omega-3 fatty acids, found in fatty fish, flaxseeds, and walnuts, have anti-inflammatory properties. Including these in the diet may help mitigate inflammation associated with IBD.

- **Probiotics and prebiotics:** Probiotics are beneficial bacteria that support gut health, while prebiotics are dietary fibers that promote the growth of these beneficial bacteria. Maintaining a balanced gut microbiome through the consumption of probiotics and prebiotics can aid in symptom management and overall well-being.

2.2. Benefits of a well-planned diet

A well-planned diet offers several benefits for individuals with IBD:

- **Improved nutrient absorption:** A diet rich in essential nutrients ensures that the body can effectively absorb and utilize these nutrients. This is especially important for IBD patients, as inflammation in the gut can hinder nutrient absorption.

- **Balanced energy levels:** Proper nutrition helps maintain energy levels, which is essential for overall health and managing the fatigue often associated with IBD.

- **Symptom control:** Dietary choices can either trigger or alleviate IBD symptoms. A well-planned diet can help in reducing symptoms such as abdominal pain, diarrhea, and bloating.

- **Gut health:** Certain foods can support a healthy gut microbiome, reducing the risk of disease flares and contributing to better digestive health.

- **Reduced risk of complications:** Managing nutrient deficiencies and promoting overall health through a balanced diet can reduce the risk of complications and comorbidities associated with IBD.

- **Quality of life:** By making informed nutritional choices, individuals with IBD can experience an improved quality of life. A well-planned diet not only helps in managing symptoms but also enhances overall well-being, allowing for a more fulfilling and active lifestyle.

2.3. Key dietary principles for managing ibd symptoms

Managing Inflammatory Bowel Disease (IBD) through dietary choices involves adhering to key principles that focus on symptom control, inflammation reduction, gut health promotion, and effective nutrient absorption.

These principles form the foundation of a well-considered diet for individuals with IBD.

2.4. Balancing inflammation

- **Anti-inflammatory foods:** Incorporating anti-inflammatory foods into the diet can help reduce gut inflammation. These foods include fatty fish rich in omega-3 fatty acids (such as salmon and mackerel), olive oil, turmeric, and ginger.
- **Fiber management:** Balancing fiber intake is crucial. Soluble fiber, found in foods like oats, bananas, and apples, can help regulate bowel movements without exacerbating symptoms, while insoluble fiber should be consumed in moderation.
- **Avoiding trigger foods:** Identifying and avoiding trigger foods that exacerbate inflammation or induce symptoms is essential. Common trigger foods in IBD include spicy foods, caffeine, alcohol, and high-fat or fried items.

2.5. Promoting gut health

- **Probiotics:** Including probiotic-rich foods like yogurt, kefir, and fermented foods in the diet can help maintain a healthy balance of gut bacteria, potentially reducing the risk of disease flares.

- **Prebiotics:** Prebiotics, found in foods like garlic, onions, and leeks, promote the growth of beneficial gut bacteria. Including prebiotic foods can support a diverse and balanced gut microbiome.

- **Hydration:** Staying adequately hydrated is essential for digestive health. Proper hydration can prevent constipation and support overall gut function.

2.6. Supporting nutrient absorption

- **Balanced diet:** Ensuring a balanced intake of macronutrients (proteins, carbohydrates, and fats) is essential. A balanced diet supports effective nutrient absorption and utilization.

- **Nutrient-dense foods:** Prioritizing nutrient-dense foods, such as lean proteins, fruits, vegetables, and whole grains, ensures that the body receives essential vitamins and minerals.

- **Supplements when necessary:** In cases of nutrient deficiencies, supplementation under the guidance of a healthcare professional may be necessary to support nutrient absorption and overall health.

- **Small, frequent meals:** Eating small, frequent meals throughout the day can help the body absorb nutrients more effectively and minimize the strain on the digestive system.

- **Individualized approach:** Recognizing that nutrient absorption can vary from person to person, an individualized dietary approach is often the most effective way to support nutrient uptake.

3. Foods to avoid or limit for better symptom management

Managing Inflammatory Bowel Disease (IBD) often involves being mindful of dietary choices. There are certain foods that individuals with IBD should consider avoiding or limiting to better manage their symptoms and reduce the risk of flares. These foods are known to be common triggers for IBD-related symptoms.

3.1 Common IBD Triggers

- **Spicy foods:** Spices and spicy foods can irritate the gastrointestinal tract and lead to increased inflammation, potentially worsening IBD symptoms.

- **Caffeine:** Beverages and foods containing caffeine, such as coffee, tea, and chocolate, can act as stimulants to the digestive system, potentially leading to diarrhea and increased gut discomfort.

- **Alcohol:** Alcohol can be harsh on the stomach and may exacerbate IBD symptoms. It can also interfere with the absorption of certain medications.

- **High-fiber foods:** Insoluble fiber found in foods like whole grains, nuts, and seeds may be difficult to digest and can lead to bowel obstructions or discomfort. Individuals with IBD should manage their fiber intake and focus on soluble fiber sources.

- **Dairy products:** Dairy products, especially for individuals with lactose intolerance, can lead to gastrointestinal distress. Lactose-free alternatives may be a better option for those with IBD.

- **Carbonated beverages:** Carbonated drinks can cause gas and bloating, which are often already common symptoms in individuals with IBD.

3.2. High-fat and processed foods

- **Fried foods:** Deep-fried and greasy foods can be problematic, as they are often high in unhealthy fats. These fats can lead to digestive discomfort and may contribute to inflammation.
- **Processed foods:** Processed foods, such as fast food, pre-packaged snacks, and sugary cereals, are often high in trans fats and artificial additives. These additives can irritate the gut and lead to worsening symptoms.
- **Saturated fats:** Foods high in saturated fats, like red meat and full-fat dairy, can increase inflammation and should be consumed in moderation.

3.3. Sugars and artificial additives

- **High-sugar foods:** Sugary foods and beverages can lead to rapid spikes and crashes in blood sugar levels, potentially aggravating IBD symptoms. Reducing sugar intake is advisable.

- **Artificial additives:** Foods containing artificial additives, such as artificial sweeteners and preservatives, can be harsh on the digestive system. Avoiding or limiting these additives is beneficial for individuals with IBD.

4. Meal planning and recipes for ibd remission

Creating meal plans that cater to individuals with Inflammatory Bowel Disease (IBD) in remission is crucial for maintaining good digestive health and overall well-being. These meal plans focus on building IBD-friendly meals and include sample meal plans as well as nutritious and delicious recipes to inspire those with IBD.

4.1. Building IBD-friendly meals

- **Lean proteins:** Incorporating lean proteins, such as skinless poultry, fish, tofu, and well-cooked eggs, can provide essential nutrients without exacerbating IBD symptoms. Proteins are a vital part of any meal.

- **Low-fiber vegetables:** Opting for cooked or peeled vegetables, such as carrots, zucchini, and butternut squash, can provide valuable vitamins and minerals while being gentle on the digestive system. Avoiding raw or high-fiber vegetables is recommended.

- **Soluble fiber:** Including soluble fiber sources like oats, white rice, and bananas can help regulate bowel movements without causing distress. These foods can be part of a well-balanced diet for individuals with IBD.

- **Good fats:** Choosing sources of good fats, such as avocados, olive oil, and nuts, can provide healthy fats that do not contribute to inflammation.

- **Low-lactose dairy:** For those who can tolerate dairy, opting for low-lactose or lactose-free dairy products like lactose-free milk, yogurt, and hard cheeses can be included in meal plans.

- **Probiotic-rich foods:** Including probiotic-rich foods like yogurt and kefir can support gut health by promoting the growth of beneficial gut bacteria.

5. Supplements and nutritional considerations

Meeting the nutritional needs of individuals with Inflammatory Bowel Disease (IBD) requires careful attention to dietary choices and, in some cases, the inclusion of supplements. Here, we explore how to meet nutritional needs and the role of supplements, with a specific focus on vitamins and minerals for IBD patients.

5.1. Meeting nutritional needs

- **Balanced diet:** A well-balanced diet that includes a variety of foods is the foundation of meeting nutritional needs for individuals with IBD. This diet should be rich in lean proteins, low-fiber vegetables, and easily digestible carbohydrates.

- **Customized plans:** Nutritional needs can vary from person to person. It is advisable for IBD patients to work with a registered dietitian or healthcare provider to create a customized nutrition plan that considers individual dietary triggers, symptoms, and nutritional deficiencies.

- **Hydration:** Staying adequately hydrated is essential for IBD patients, as diarrhea and fluid loss can lead to dehydration. Drinking plenty of water and, in some cases, oral rehydration solutions can help maintain proper hydration.

- **Fiber management:** For individuals with IBD, particularly during active flares, managing fiber intake is vital. While soluble fiber can be beneficial, insoluble fiber, found in foods like whole grains and raw vegetables, should be limited.

- **Food diary:** Keeping a food diary can help individuals track their dietary choices in relation to symptom flares. This practice can identify trigger foods and inform dietary adjustments.

5.2. The role of supplements

- **Multivitamins:** In some cases, IBD patients may require a daily multivitamin to ensure they receive a broad spectrum of essential nutrients. Multivitamins can help compensate for potential nutrient deficiencies.

- **Calcium and vitamin D:** Many individuals with IBD are at risk of calcium and vitamin D deficiencies, especially if they are lactose intolerant or avoid dairy products. Calcium and vitamin D supplements may be recommended to support bone health.

- **Iron:** Chronic intestinal bleeding or malabsorption can lead to iron deficiencies in IBD patients. Iron supplements, under the guidance of a healthcare provider, can help manage anemia.

- **B12 and Folate:** Individuals with Crohn's disease that affects the ileum may have difficulty absorbing vitamin B12. In such cases, B12 injections or supplements may be necessary. Folate supplementation may also be considered.

- **Omega-3 Fatty Acids:** Omega-3 fatty acid supplements, such as fish oil, can have anti-inflammatory properties and may be beneficial for managing IBD symptoms.

- **Probiotics:** Probiotic supplements contain beneficial bacteria that can support gut health. While research on their effectiveness for IBD is ongoing, some individuals find probiotics helpful.

5.3. Vitamins and minerals

- **Vitamin A:** Important for immune function and skin health. Individuals with IBD may require supplementation if they have difficulty absorbing fat-soluble vitamins.

- **Vitamin C:** Supports the immune system and wound healing. A diet rich in fruits and vegetables can provide adequate vitamin C.

- **Vitamin E:** An antioxidant that may help reduce inflammation. Nuts, seeds, and spinach are good dietary sources.

- **Zinc:** Essential for immune function and wound healing. Zinc supplements may be recommended for individuals with deficiencies.

- **Magnesium:** Important for muscle and nerve function. Magnesium supplements may be necessary for those with deficiencies.

- **Potassium:** Necessary for heart and muscle function. Individuals with IBD at risk of potassium deficiencies may require supplements.

6. Seeking professional guidance: dietitians and IBD remission

Managing Inflammatory Bowel Disease (IBD) during remission involves a thoughtful approach to diet and nutrition. Seeking professional guidance from dietitians who specialize in IBD can make a significant difference in understanding the complexities of dietary management. Here, we explore the expertise of dietitians, the benefits of working with a registered dietitian, and the development of personalized nutrition plans.

6.1. The expertise of dietitians

- **Nutritional knowledge:** Dietitians possess extensive knowledge of nutrition and its role in health, making them well-equipped to address the unique dietary considerations of IBD patients.

- **Understanding IBD:** Dietitians specializing in IBD have a deep understanding of the condition, including its symptoms, triggers, and the impact of diet on disease management.

- **Dietary triggers:** They can identify potential dietary triggers that worsen symptoms, such as high-fiber foods, lactose, or certain food groups, and help patients avoid or limit these triggers.

- **Nutritional deficiencies:** Dietitians can assess and address potential nutritional deficiencies that may result from IBD, ensuring patients receive the necessary vitamins and minerals.

6.2. Working with a registered dietitian

- **Individual assessment:** A registered dietitian conducts a comprehensive assessment of the individual's medical history, current symptoms, dietary preferences, and lifestyle to tailor recommendations

- **Personalized guidance:** Dietitians create personalized nutrition plans that consider the patient's specific needs, helping them manage their condition effectively.

- **Monitoring and adjustments:** They monitor the patient's progress, making adjustments to the nutrition plan as needed to ensure it remains in line with IBD management goals.

- **Education and empowerment:** Dietitians educate patients about their dietary choices and empower them to make informed decisions regarding their food intake.

- **Meal planning:** They assist in meal planning, offering suggestions for IBD-friendly recipes and food choices that align with the patient's dietary restrictions.

6.3. Personalized nutrition plans

- **Dietary triggers identification:** A dietitian helps identify and avoid dietary triggers that exacerbate IBD symptoms. These triggers can be unique to each patient.

- **Balanced diet:** Personalized nutrition plans aim to create a well-balanced diet that provides essential nutrients without causing inflammation or discomfort.

- **Food sensitivities:** Dietitians can help patients uncover specific food sensitivities or intolerances, allowing for a more tailored diet.

- **Supplement recommendations:** If necessary, dietitians may recommend appropriate supplements to address potential nutrient deficiencies.

- **Goal-oriented plans:** Nutrition plans are aligned with the patient's goals, whether it's symptom management, weight maintenance, or achieving optimal nutrient intake.

- **Regular follow-up:** Dietitians maintain regular follow-up appointments to track progress and make any necessary adjustments to the nutrition plan.

7. Maintaining long-term IBD remission through diet

Sustaining long-term remission of Inflammatory Bowel Disease (IBD) is a multifaceted endeavor, and diet plays a crucial role in this journey. In this section, we delve into strategies for long-term success, the need for adapting to changing dietary needs, and the ongoing role of diet in IBD care.

7.1. Strategies for long-term success

- **Consistency:** Consistency in adhering to dietary guidelines is key for maintaining long-term remission. Avoiding trigger foods and sticking to a well-balanced diet can help prevent symptom flares.

- **Regular monitoring:** Periodic check-ins with healthcare providers and dietitians are essential. Regular monitoring of nutritional status, dietary adherence, and potential triggers allows for timely adjustments.

- **Understanding individual needs:** Recognizing that each IBD patient is unique, it's important to have a deep understanding of one's individual dietary needs. This understanding may evolve over time.

- **Gradual introduction of foods:** When transitioning from flare management to remission, the reintroduction of certain foods should be gradual and carefully monitored to assess tolerance.

- **Mindful eating:** Practicing mindful eating involves being present during meals, chewing food thoroughly, and eating in a relaxed environment. This approach can promote digestion and reduce discomfort.

7.2 Adapting to changing needs

- **Aging and IBD:** As individuals with IBD age, their dietary needs and tolerance may change. Adjustments should be made to accommodate age-related factors and potential comorbidities.

- **Pregnancy and reproductive health:** For female patients of childbearing age, maintaining remission and supporting reproductive health can be intertwined. Dietary adjustments during pregnancy may be necessary.

- **Post-surgery:** Patients who have undergone surgical interventions may have different dietary requirements following the procedure. Adjusting to these changes is vital for long-term health.

- **Stress management:** Adapting to stressors in life is an ongoing challenge for IBD patients. Learning stress-reduction techniques can complement dietary strategies in maintaining remission.

7.3. The ongoing role of diet in ibd care

- **Patient-centered approach:** Recognizing that dietary preferences and tolerances may shift over time, a patient-centered approach is essential. This approach involves continuous collaboration with healthcare providers to tailor dietary plans to evolving needs.

- **Balancing nutritional and symptomatic goals:** Dietary management should balance the nutritional requirements of the body with symptom management. This ongoing balance is crucial for sustained remission.

- **Regular consultations:** IBD patients should continue to have regular consultations with healthcare providers and dietitians to address changing dietary needs and optimize overall health.

- **Community and support:** Engaging with the IBD community and support networks can provide insights, encouragement, and practical advice for maintaining remission.

- **Staying informed:** Staying informed about emerging dietary research and management strategies is important. The landscape of IBD care continually evolves, offering new possibilities for long-term success.

8. Conclusions

Diet plays a significant role in the management of Inflammatory Bowel Disease (IBD), with a focus on achieving and maintaining remission. A remission diet aims to reduce inflammation, control symptoms, promote gut healing, balance the gut microbiome, support nutrient absorption, and improve the overall quality of life for individuals with IBD. Nutritional choices, including macronutrients, micronutrients, fibre, omega-3 fatty acids, and probiotics, have a profound impact on IBD management.

Avoiding or limiting certain trigger foods, high-fat and processed foods, sugars, artificial additives, and other common IBD triggers is essential for symptom management. Building IBD-friendly meals involves lean proteins, low-fiber vegetables, soluble fiber, good fats, and probiotic-rich foods.Meeting nutritional needs often requires an individualized approach, working with a registered dietitian, and considering supplements, when necessary, especially for vitamins and minerals. Dietitians provide expertise in IBD management, create personalized nutrition plans, and offer ongoing support.

Maintaining long-term remission through diet involves consistency, regular monitoring, understanding individual needs, and adapting to changing dietary requirements over time. The patient-centered approach, balancing nutritional and symptomatic goals, regular consultations, community support, and staying informed about the latest research are all crucial components of long-term IBD care.

References

1. Loftus, E. V. (2016). Clinical epidemiology of inflammatory bowel disease: Incidence, prevalence, and environmental influences. Gastroenterology, 150(6), 1249-1258.

2. Hou, J. K., Lee, D., & Lewis, J. (2014). Diet and inflammatory bowel disease: Review of patient-targeted recommendations. Clinical Gastroenterology and Hepatology, 12(10), 1592-1600.

3. Ananthakrishnan, A. N., Khalili, H., Konijeti, G. G., Higuchi, L. M., de Silva, P., Fuchs, C. S., ... & Chan, A. T. (2014). Long-term intake of dietary fat and risk of ulcerative colitis and Crohn's disease. Gut, 63(5), 776-784.

4. Crohn's & Colitis Foundation. (n.d.). Recipe and meal planning. https://www.crohnscolitisfoundation.org/diet-and-nutrition/meal-planning

5. National Institutes of Health (NIH). (2022). Dietary Supplement Fact Sheet: Omega-3 Fatty Acids. https://ods.od.nih.gov/factsheets/Omega3FattyAcids-HealthProfessional/

6. Academy of Nutrition and Dietetics. (2022). Find an Expert Registered Dietitian Nutritionist. https://www.eatright.org/find-an-expert

7. Crohn's & Colitis Foundation. (n.d.). Living with Crohn's & Colitis. https://www.crohnscolitisfoundation.org/living-with-crohns-colitis

7.

Use of Micro-Organisms in Prevention and Treatment of Inflammatroy Bowel Diseses.

Dr. Rosy Kumari

Assistant Professor,

Department of Home Science,

Patna Women's College,

Patna University (Autonomous), Bihar, India

Email: angelrosy1991@gmail.com

Abstract

The human gut microbiome, comprising trillions of microorganisms, plays a pivotal role in maintaining health. This article explores the intricate relationship between the gut microbiome and Inflammatory Bowel Disease (IBD), encompassing conditions like Crohn's disease and ulcerative colitis. The complex interplay of genetic, immune, environmental, and microbial factors contributes to the development and progression of IBD. Alterations in the gut microbiome, such as reduced diversity, shifts in microbial composition, and the presence of pathogenic bacteria, are associated with chronic inflammation in IBD. The multifaceted nature of IBD demands personalized approaches to its management.

The article delves into various strategies to harness the potential of microorganisms for IBD management. Probiotics, fecal microbiota transplantation (FMT), and prebiotics emerge as promising interventions, aiming to restore a balanced and diverse gut microbiome. Dietary interventions, including the low-FODMAP diet, Specific Carbohydrate Diet (SCD), and plant-based diets, play a significant role in alleviating IBD symptoms. The gut microbiome's impact on digestion, nutrient absorption, immune regulation, and protection against pathogens is explored, highlighting its vital role in overall health.

Looking toward the future, precision medicine approaches tailored to individual microbiome profiles and further exploration of microbial therapies offer exciting possibilities. However, challenges such as the complexity of IBD, heterogeneity in patient presentations, and regulatory considerations for microbial therapies must be addressed. The evolving field holds promise for personalized and effective treatments, offering hope for an improved quality of life for individuals living with IBD.

Keywords: Gut microbiome, Inflammatory Bowel Disease (IBD), Crohn's disease, Ulcerative Colitis, Fecal microbiota transplantation (FMT), prebiotics, Dietary Interventions.

1. Introduction

The human gut is home to trillions of microorganisms, collectively known as the gut microbiome, which plays a pivotal role in maintaining our health. In recent years, extensive research has been conducted to better understand the intricate relationship between the gut microbiome and various health conditions, including Inflammatory Bowel Disease (IBD). This article delves into the fascinating world of gut microorganisms, their role in IBD, and the various strategies used to harness their potential for IBD management.

The role of microorganisms in the gut, collectively referred to as the gut microbiome, is a multifaceted and crucial aspect of human health. This complex community of microorganisms, which includes bacteria, viruses, fungi, and other microbes, resides in the gastrointestinal tract and has a profound impact on various aspects of our well-being. Here's an explanation of the key roles these microorganisms play in the gut:

2. Inflammatory bowel disease

Inflammatory Bowel Disease (IBD) represents a chronic inflammatory condition affecting the gastrointestinal tract (GI), characterized by structural disruptions in the mucosa, changes in the composition of gut microbes, and systemic biochemical irregularities. It manifests in two primary clinical forms: ulcerative colitis (UC) and Crohn's disease (CD), distinguished by variations in inflammation patterns and the location of intestinal involvement.

Over the last decade, IBD has emerged as a significant global public health concern, with its incidence progressively rising worldwide. Developed regions like North America, Europe, Australia, and NewZealand have reported the highest rates of incidence. However, more recently, IBD is increasingly becoming prevalent in areas that were previously less affected, including parts of Asia and South America. Developing countries such as Brazil, South Korea, and China have witnessed a gradual increase in the prevalence of IBD. This suggests a shifting trend in the geographical distribution of IBD, with its impact expanding beyond traditionally high-incidence regions.Inflammatory bowel disease is a term used for ulcerative colitis and Crohn's disease. Both may have the related condition of short bowel syndrome if there have been re- peated surgeries that removed sections of the bowel as the disease progressed.

Both ulcerative colitis (UC) and Crohn's disease have increased in incidence in the United States. They have similar pathophysiology and clinical symptoms, but are prevalent in different groups. They both have severe nu- tritional consequences, but are separate diseases. Crohn's can occur anywhere in the GI tract, but UC is confined to the colon and rectum. The pattern of disease in Crohn's is that of a chronic disorder, often involving the entire in- testinal wall. This may cause complications, such as par- tial or complete obstruction and the formation of fistulas. The inflammatory processes in UC, on the other hand, are usually acute and are limited to the mucosa and submucosa of the intestine. The patient may have periods of remission. Diet therapy for inflammatory bowel disease is based upon the common clinical symptoms of bloody diarrhea and the various associated nutritional problems.

3. Etiology

The etiology of Inflammatory Bowel Disease (IBD), including ulcerative colitis (UC) and Crohn's disease (CD), is complex and multifactorial, involving a combination of genetic, environmental, immune system, and microbial factors.

3.1. Genetic factors

There is a substantial genetic component to IBD. Multiple genetic variations have been identified that predispose individuals to IBD, making them more susceptible to developing the condition. These genetic factors can influence how the immune system responds to the gut microbiota and the environment.

3.2. Immune system dysregulation

The immune system plays a crucial role in IBD. In individuals with IBD, the immune system's response in the gastrointestinal tract becomes overactive, leading to chronic inflammation. The body's immune cells mistakenly attack the intestinal lining, causing continuous inflammation and damage.

3.3. Environmental triggers

Environmental factors are believed to contribute significantly to the development and exacerbation of

IBD. Factors such as diet, smoking, infections, antibiotic use, stress, and other environmental exposures might influence the onset or progression of the disease. Changes in diet, for instance, can impact the gut microbiota, which in turn affects the immune response and inflammation in the gut.

3.4. Gut microbiota

The collection of microorganisms residing in the gut, known as the gut microbiota, also plays a role in IBD. Changes in the composition or diversity of these microbes can influence the immune response and inflammation in the gut. An imbalance in the gut microbiota, known as dysbiosis, can trigger or exacerbate inflammation in IBD.

3.5. Mucosal barrier dysfunction

In IBD, there's a breakdown in the protective mucosal barrier lining the intestine, allowing harmful substances to come into contact with the immune system. This breach in the barrier contributes to the perpetuation of inflammation.

The interplay among these factors—genetic predisposition, immune system dysfunction, environmental influences, alterations in the gut microbiota, and mucosal barrier dysfunction—contributes to the development and progression of IBD. The specific combination of these factors may vary among individuals, which is why the manifestation and severity of IBD can differ greatly from person to person. Understanding and addressing these multifaceted factors is crucial in the management and treatment of IBD.

4. Ulcerative colitis and crohn's disease

Ulcerative Colitis (UC) and Crohn's Disease are health problems that affect the digestive system. UC is more common in young adults, especially women, and it can be quite serious. The exact cause is unknown, but stress and psychological factors may play a role. It leads to widespread inflammation and sores in the colon, causing symptoms like fever, chronic bloody diarrhea, swelling, and anemia. People with UC often become malnourished and suffer from various health issues.Crohn's Disease is another type of digestive problem and is more common in industrial areas and among people aged 55 to 60. It starts slowly and causes pain, tenderness, and cramping in the lower right part of the bowel. While there is less blood in the stool compared to UC, there is an increased production of mucus. Crohn's can affect the small bowel, leading to problems like weight loss, anemia, and deficiencies in vitamins and minerals.Both UC and Crohn's can result in the body not absorbing essential nutrients properly. This can lead to various complications like vitamin deficiencies, anemia, and problems with bones and nerves. For example, the lack of certain vitamins can cause issues like bleeding, skin problems, and nerve damage. Children with Crohn's might experience slower growth.To treat these conditions, a proper diet is crucial. The goal is to replenish the nutrients the body is lacking, prevent further losses, and support the healing and maintenance of the body tissues. It's important to address these nutritional issues to improve the overall health of individuals with UC or Crohn's Disease.

5. Digestion and nutrient absorption

The gut microbiome contributes significantly to the digestion of dietary components that our own enzymes cannot break down. Certain microorganisms are capable of metabolizing complex carbohydrates, fibers, and other substrates, producing short-chain fatty acids (SCFAs) as byproducts. SCFAs are essential for energy production and promoting the health of intestinal cells. Furthermore, the gut microbiome aids in the absorption of essential nutrients, including certain vitamins and minerals.

6. Immune system regulation

The gut microbiome plays a pivotal role in regulating the immune system. It helps train the immune system to distinguish between beneficial and harmful substances, ensuring that the immune response is appropriate. When this balance is disrupted, as in conditions like Inflammatory Bowel Disease (IBD), the immune system may become dysregulated, leading to chronic inflammation.

7. Protection against pathogens

A diverse and healthy gut microbiome acts as a barrier against invading pathogens. Beneficial microorganisms can outcompete harmful ones for resources and attachment sites in the gut lining. They also produce antimicrobial substances that inhibit the growth of pathogenic bacteria. This defense mechanism helps prevent infections and maintains gut health.

8. Synthesis of bioactive compounds

Certain gut bacteria are capable of synthesizing bioactive compounds, such as vitamins (e.g., vitamin K, B vitamins) and neurotransmitters (e.g., serotonin), which have far-reaching effects on our overall health. These compounds can influence various physiological processes, including blood clotting, mood regulation, and gut motility.

9. Metabolic health

The gut microbiome has been linked to metabolic health, including the regulation of body weight and metabolism. It can influence how the body stores and utilizes energy from food. An imbalance in the gut microbiome has been associated with conditions like obesity and metabolic syndrome.

10. Gut-brain axis

Emerging research suggests a strong connection between the gut and the brain, known as the gut-brain axis. The gut microbiome can produce neurotransmitters and communicate with the central nervous system, influencing mood, behavior, and cognitive function. Disruptions in the gut microbiome have been linked to mental health disorders like depression and anxiety.

11. Gut barrier integrity

The gut microbiome contributes to the maintenance of the gut barrier, which is essential for preventing the leakage of harmful substances from the gut into the bloodstream. A disrupted gut barrier, often referred to as "leaky gut," has been associated with various autoimmune and inflammatory conditions.

12. Drug metabolism

Certain gut bacteria can metabolize drugs and other xenobiotics, potentially impacting their efficacy and safety. Understanding these interactions is essential for personalized medicine and drug development.

The gut microbiome is a dynamic ecosystem that exerts a profound influence on human health and well-being. Maintaining a balanced and diverse gut microbiome is critical for optimal digestion, immune function, metabolic health, and even mental well-being. As our understanding of the gut microbiome continues to grow, so does the potential for innovative approaches to improve health and treat a wide range of medical conditions

13. The gut microbiome in IBD

In IBD, which encompasses conditions like Crohn's disease and ulcerative colitis, the gut microbiome undergoes significant alterations. These changes can include a reduction in microbial diversity, shifts in the relative abundance of specific microbial species, and an increase in pathogenic bacteria. These alterations are thought to contribute to the chronic inflammation characteristic of IBD.

Inflammatory Bowel Disease (IBD) is a group of chronic gastrointestinal disorders that includes conditions like Crohn's disease and ulcerative colitis. In these conditions, the gut microbiome undergoes notable changes, which have been a subject of extensive research and are thought to play a crucial role in the development and progression of IBD. Here's an explanation of these alterations and their significance:

13.1. Reduction in microbial diversity

In individuals with IBD, there is often a noticeable decrease in the diversity of the gut microbiome. This means that the number and variety of different microbial species present in the gut are reduced. A diverse microbiome is generally considered a sign of a healthy gut. Reduced diversity is associated with a less resilient gut ecosystem, making it more vulnerable to disturbances and less capable of performing its various functions effectively.

13.2. Shifts in microbial composition

Along with reduced diversity, there are specific shifts in the relative abundance of microbial species within the gut. Some beneficial or commensal (mutually beneficial) bacteria may decrease in number, while potentially harmful bacteria may increase in abundance. These imbalances can disrupt the equilibrium of the gut microbiome and may contribute to the inflammatory processes seen in IBD.

13.3. Increase in pathogenic bacteria

In IBD, there is often an overgrowth of potentially pathogenic bacteria in the gut. These bacteria may include species that are known to trigger inflammatory responses and damage the intestinal lining. Such overgrowth can further exacerbate inflammation and lead to a continuous cycle of immune responses and tissue damage.

13.4. Chronic inflammation

The chronic inflammation characteristic of IBD is a result of an inappropriate and sustained immune response in the gut. This inflammation can cause damage to the intestinal lining and result in symptoms like abdominal pain, diarrhea, and rectal bleeding. The changes in the gut microbiome, particularly the increase in pathogenic bacteria and the imbalance of microbial species, are believed to trigger and perpetuate this inflammation.

Researchers are actively studying these alterations in the gut microbiome to understand their exact role in IBD. It's important to note that the relationship between the gut microbiome and IBD is complex and multifactorial. While these microbial changes are associated with IBD, it's not yet fully understood whether they are the primary cause or a consequence of the disease. Nevertheless, the gut microbiome is a promising area for potential IBD treatments, with interventions like probiotics, fecal microbiota transplantation (FMT), and dietary modifications aimed at restoring a healthier microbial balance and reducing inflammation in the gut.

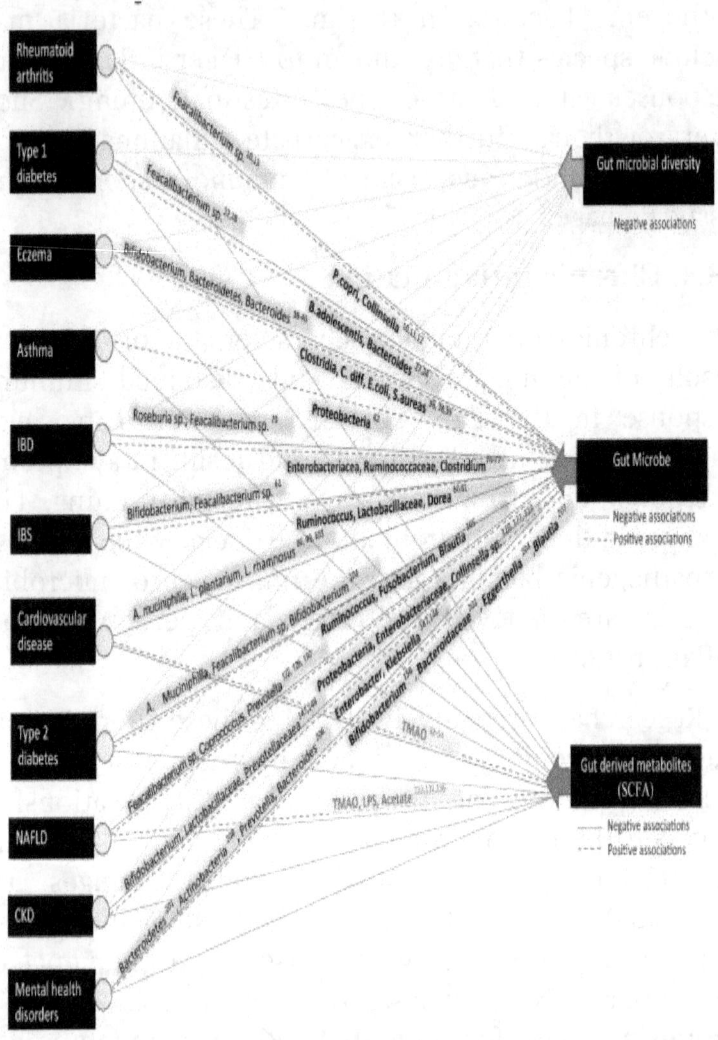

Fig. 1.1.1: Schematic representation of the association of the composition of the gut microbiome and gut-derived metabolites with chronic diseases.

Source: https://www.nature.com/articles/s41430-021-00991-6

(The solid lines represent negative associations and the dashed lines represent positive associations of the disease phenotype with gut microbes and metabolites)

14. Use of microorganisms in IBD

Researchers and healthcare providers have explored various ways to manipulate the gut microbiome to mitigate the symptoms of IBD and improve the overall health of individuals with these conditions. Some of the key strategies include:

The use of microorganisms in Inflammatory Bowel Disease (IBD) represents a promising avenue for managing the condition. Researchers and healthcare providers have explored several strategies to manipulate the gut microbiome in an effort to mitigate the symptoms of IBD and improve the overall health of individuals with these conditions. An explanation of some of the key strategies are given in Fig. 1.1.1.

The composition of the gut microbiome (the community of microorganisms in the digestive tract) and the metabolites they produce play a critical role in human health. Research suggests that an imbalance in the gut microbiome, known as dysbiosis, can lead to the production of certain metabolites associated with chronic diseases.

For instance, an altered gut microbiome composition can produce metabolites that contribute to inflammation, insulin resistance, and metabolic disorders. These metabolites might affect the immune system, leading to conditions such as inflammatory bowel disease, obesity, diabetes, cardiovascular diseases, and even neurological disorders like Parkinson's and Alzheimer's.

The specific metabolites involved in these diseases can vary, but certain byproducts like short-chain fatty acids, trimethylamine N-oxide (TMAO), and various neurotransmitters might play roles in disease development or progression.

Understanding and potentially manipulating the gut microbiome and its metabolites could offer new insights into preventing or managing chronic diseases, potentially through dietary interventions, probiotics, or targeted therapies to restore a healthier balance in the gut.

15. Probiotics in IBD

Probiotics are live microorganisms, primarily beneficial bacteria, that can be consumed in various forms, such as capsules, yogurt, or other food products. When taken in sufficient quantities, they are believed to confer health benefits by positively affecting the gut microbiome. Probiotics are used as safe food additives, pharmaceutical formulations or nutritional supplements defined as "live microorganisms which, when administered in adequate amounts, confer a health benefit on the host" by the World Health Organization (WHO).

15.1. Role in IBD

Probiotics have been investigated in IBD for their potential to modulate the gut microbiome and immune response. Specific strains of probiotics have shown promise in reducing inflammation and alleviating symptoms in some individuals with IBD. They can help restore a healthier microbial balance and improve gut barrier function.

16. Fecal microbiota transplantation (FMT)

FMT involves transferring fecal material from a healthy donor into the gut of a person with IBD. This procedure aims to restore a balanced and diverse gut microbiome by introducing a wide range of beneficial microorganisms.

16.1. Role in IBD

FMT has gained recognition for its remarkable success in treating recurrent Clostridium difficile infection. In the context of IBD, research is ongoing to determine its safety and efficacy. FMT may offer a way to reset the gut microbiome and reduce inflammation, providing potential relief for some IBD patients.

17. Prebiotics

Prebiotics are non-digestible compounds, often dietary fibers, that serve as a food source for beneficial gut bacteria. They encourage the growth and activity of beneficial microorganisms in the gut.

17.1. Role in IBD

Prebiotics have been studied for their potential to promote a healthier gut microbiome in IBD patients. By increasing the population of beneficial microbes, prebiotics can potentially reduce inflammation, enhance the gut barrier, and improve overall gut health. However, individual responses to prebiotics may vary.

These strategies aim to address the gut dysbiosis, or microbial imbalance, often observed in individuals with IBD. By restoring a more balanced and diverse gut microbiome, it is hoped that the chronic inflammation and symptoms of IBD can be mitigated. However, it's essential to understand that the effectiveness of these interventions may vary from person to person, and not all individuals with IBD will experience the same benefits.

IBD is a complex condition with multiple factors at play, and while manipulating the gut microbiome is a promising approach, it is often used in combination with other therapies to manage the disease effectively. Additionally, ongoing research is essential to better understand the specific microbial imbalances and how to tailor microbial interventions for individual patients

Dietary interventions play a significant role in IBD management. Certain diets, such as the low-FODMAP diet, Specific Carbohydrate Diet (SCD), or the Mediterranean diet, have been explored for their potential to reduce symptoms and improve the quality of life for individuals with IBD. These diets often incorporate prebiotic-rich foods to support a healthier gut microbiome.

18. Dietary interventions and their impact on IBD

A variety of dietary interventions have been studied in IBD, ranging from eliminating specific trigger foods to adopting more plant-based diets or consuming fermented foods. The impact of these dietary changes can vary from person to person, highlighting the need for personalized dietary guidance for IBD patients.

Dietary interventions play a significant role in managing Inflammatory Bowel Disease (IBD), which includes conditions like Crohn's disease and ulcerative colitis. These dietary strategies aim to alleviate symptoms, reduce inflammation, and improve the overall well-being of individuals with IBD. Here's an explanation of various dietary interventions and their impact on IBD:

19. Elimination of trigger foods

Many IBD patients identify specific trigger foods that exacerbate their symptoms. These trigger foods can vary from person to person and may include items like dairy products, high-fiber foods, spicy foods, or certain fats. Eliminating these triggers is a common approach.

Impact: Eliminating trigger foods can help reduce the frequency and severity of symptom flares, such as abdominal pain, diarrhea, and cramping. However, it's essential to work with a healthcare provider or dietitian to identify individual triggers and ensure that the diet remains balanced and nutritionally adequate.

20. LOW-FODMAP diet

The Low-FODMAP diet restricts certain types of carbohydrates (Fermentable Oligosaccharides, Disaccharides, Monosaccharides, and Polyols) that are known to cause gastrointestinal symptoms in some people. This diet can be especially helpful for those with IBD who experience excessive gas, bloating, and diarrhea.

IMPACT: The Low-FODMAP diet can reduce gastrointestinal symptoms, making it easier to manage IBD. However, it should be undertaken with the guidance of a healthcare provider or registered dietitian to ensure that essential nutrients are not compromised.

21. Specific carbohydrate diet (SCD) and similar diets

Diets like the Specific Carbohydrate Diet (SCD) and the GAPS (Gut and Psychology Syndrome) diet restrict the intake of complex carbohydrates and grains, emphasizing whole foods, lean protein, and some fruits and vegetables.

Impact: These diets may reduce inflammation and symptoms in some individuals with IBD. However, they are restrictive and require close monitoring to ensure balanced nutrition and prevent potential deficiencies.

22. Plant-based diet

A plant-based diet emphasizes fruits, vegetables, whole grains, and legumes while minimizing or eliminating animal products. It is rich in fiber, antioxidants, and anti-inflammatory compounds.

Impact: Some IBD patients find relief from symptoms by adopting a plant-based diet. The high fiber content can promote gut health and reduce inflammation. However, individual responses may vary.

23. Consumption of fermented foods

Fermented foods, such as yogurt, kefir, kimchi, and sauerkraut, contain beneficial probiotic bacteria. These foods can contribute to a healthier gut microbiome.

Impact: Including fermented foods in the diet may help support a balanced gut microbiome and reduce inflammation. However, their effectiveness can differ from person to person.

It's crucial to recognize that IBD is a highly individualized condition, and what works for one person may not work for another. Personalized dietary guidance is essential for IBD patients to determine which dietary interventions are most suitable for their specific needs and to monitor their nutritional status. Working closely with healthcare providers and registered dietitians can help individuals with IBD make informed decisions about their dietary choices and achieve the best outcomes in symptom management and overall health. Additionally, it's important to consider that dietary interventions are often used in conjunction with medical treatments to comprehensively manage IBD.

24. Future directions and challenges

The relationship between the gut microbiome and IBD is complex and multifaceted, and ongoing research is needed to fully understand the role of microorganisms in the development and progression of IBD. Future directions may include the development of precision medicine approaches tailored to individual microbiome profiles, further exploration of microbial therapies, and better elucidation of the long-term effects of dietary interventions on IBD.

The future of understanding and managing Inflammatory Bowel Disease (IBD) is characterized by both exciting possibilities and ongoing challenges. The relationship between the gut microbiome and IBD is indeed complex and multifaceted, and research continues to evolve in this area. Here's an explanation of the future directions and challenges in IBD research and management:

25. Precision medicine approaches

The concept of precision medicine involves tailoring medical treatments, including dietary and microbial interventions, to an individual's unique characteristics, such as their genetic makeup, gut microbiome profile, and disease history. In the context of IBD, this approach could lead to more personalized and effective therapies.

Impact: Precision medicine has the potential to revolutionize IBD management by identifying specific microbial imbalances, genetic factors, and other individualized aspects that contribute to the disease. It can help match the right treatment to the right patient, optimizing outcomes and minimizing side effects.

26. Microbial therapies

Microbial therapies, including probiotics, prebiotics, and fecal microbiota transplantation (FMT), represent an emerging area of interest. Researchers are investigating specific microbial strains and formulations that can modulate the gut microbiome to reduce inflammation and alleviate IBD symptoms.

Impact: As our understanding of the gut microbiome advances, the development of targeted microbial therapies becomes more promising. These therapies can potentially offer alternative or complementary treatments to conventional medications, providing new options for IBD patients.

27. long-term effects of dietary interventions

Dietary interventions, such as specific diets or the consumption of certain foods, have shown promise in managing IBD. However, it is essential to comprehensively understand the long-term effects of these dietary changes on gut health and overall well-being.

Impact: Future research will need to investigate the sustainability and safety of dietary interventions. A better understanding of how these interventions affect the gut microbiome, nutrient absorption, and disease progression over time will inform more effective dietary recommendations for IBD patients.

28. Challenges

28.1. Complexity of IBD

IBD is a multifaceted condition with various contributing factors, including genetic, environmental, and microbial influences. Understanding how these factors interact and trigger inflammation is a considerable challenge.

28.2. Heterogeneity

IBD presents differently in different individuals, making it challenging to develop one-size-fits-all treatments. Tailoring treatments to the individual patient is crucial, but it adds complexity to diagnosis and management.

Safety and Efficacy: Ensuring the safety and efficacy of microbial therapies, especially FMT, is an ongoing challenge. Balancing the potential benefits with the risk of unintended consequences or complications is vital.

28.3. Regulatory and ethical considerations

The use of microbial therapies, particularly FMT, raises regulatory and ethical questions regarding donor screening, standardization of treatments, and long-term follow-up.

The future of IBD research and management is characterized by a dynamic landscape with promising opportunities for personalized, effective treatments. However, there are still many challenges to address, including the need for rigorous research, regulatory oversight, and ethical considerations in the field of microbial therapies. As our understanding of the gut microbiome and IBD deepens, there is hope for improved outcomes and quality of life for individuals living with these challenging conditions

The gut microbiome's role in IBD is a dynamic and evolving field of research. While there is no one-size-fits-all solution, harnessing the power of microorganisms through probiotics, FMT, and prebiotics, along with carefully tailored dietary interventions, holds promise for managing IBD and improving the lives of those affected by these challenging conditions. As our understanding of the gut microbiome and IBD continues to expand, the potential for innovative and effective treatments grows, offering hope for a brighter future for IBD patients.

The conclusion highlights the evolving and promising nature of research into the role of the gut microbiome in Inflammatory Bowel Disease (IBD). Here's an explanation of the key points in the conclusion:

28.4. Dynamic field of research

The gut microbiome's involvement in IBD is a subject of ongoing investigation and is characterized by its dynamic and evolving nature. Researchers are continuously uncovering new insights into how microorganisms in the gut contribute to the development and progression of IBD.

28.5. No one-size-fits-all solution

IBD is a complex condition with significant individual variability. There is no single, universal solution that works for every IBD patient. What may benefit one individual might not work as effectively for another. As such, personalized approaches are crucial in IBD management.

28.6. Harnessing microorganisms

The conclusion highlights the potential of harnessing microorganisms, such as probiotics, FMT, and prebiotics, to manage IBD. These approaches aim to restore a healthier balance to the gut microbiome, reduce inflammation, and alleviate symptoms. These methods represent promising options for many IBD patients.

28.7. Tailored dietary interventions

Dietary interventions are recognized as an integral part of IBD management. These dietary changes can include avoiding trigger foods, adopting specific diets, or incorporating foods that promote gut health. The key is to tailor dietary recommendations to the individual needs and sensitivities of each IBD patient.

28.8. Expanding understanding

As our understanding of the gut microbiome and IBD deepens, the potential for innovative and effective treatments continues to grow. This suggests that there is hope on the horizon for individuals affected by IBD. Advances in research may lead to more targeted and successful therapies.

In summary, the conclusion emphasizes the optimism surrounding the potential for improved management of IBD by focusing on the gut microbiome. While challenges remain, ongoing research is likely to uncover new approaches and treatments that can enhance the lives of those dealing with the complexities of IBD. This offers hope for a brighter future for IBD patients, with the prospect of more personalized and effective strategies to manage their condition and improve their overall well-being.

29. Conclusions

In conclusion, the dynamic field of research surrounding the gut microbiome and Inflammatory Bowel Disease (IBD) offers optimism for improved management strategies. Recognizing the individualized nature of IBD, there is no one-size-fits-all solution, emphasizing the need for personalized approaches. Harnessing the potential of microorganisms through probiotics, FMT, and prebiotics, along with carefully tailored dietary interventions, holds promise for managing IBD and enhancing the lives of affected individuals.

The importance of ongoing research is highlighted, focusing on precision medicine approaches, microbial therapies, and understanding the long-term effects of dietary interventions. Challenges, including the complexity of IBD, patient heterogeneity, and regulatory considerations, must be addressed. As our understanding deepens, the potential for innovative and effective treatments grows, offering hope for a brighter future for IBD patients. The combination of advancements in research and personalized care holds the key to optimizing outcomes and improving the overall well-being of individuals navigating the complexities of IBD.

References

1. Hill C., Guarner F., Reid G., Gibson G. R., Merenstein D. J., Pot B., *et al.*(2014) Expert consensus document. The International Scientific Association for Probiotics and Prebiotics consensus statement on the scope and appropriate use of the term probiotic. *Nat. Rev. Gastroenterol. Hepatol.* 11 506–514. 10.1038/nrgastro.2014.66.

2. Amrita Vijay and Ana M. Valdes (2021) Role of the gut microbiome in chronic diseases: a narrative review. European journal of clinical nutrition 76 Page No. 489–501. https://www.nature.com/articles/s41430-021-00991-6

3. F.P. Antia and Philip Abraham4[th] Edition Clinical Dietetics and nutrition, fourth edition. Oxford University Press. ISBN-10: 0-19-56641-9. Page No. 290-294 www.oup.com

8.

Paediatric IBD Compass: Navigating the Landscape of Care and Resilience

Arushi Jain

Research scholar

Lady Irwin College

University of Delhi

Email: arushijain709@gmail.com

Abstract

The management of paediatric Inflammatory Bowel Disease (IBD) requires a multifaceted approach that addresses both the medical and nutritional aspects unique to children. This chapter provides a comprehensive overview of the complexities involved in understanding, managing, and supporting children with IBD along with the medical nutritional therapy. It provides a brief overview of paediatric IBD, emphasizing the need for specialized attention to the challenges faced by young patients. Acknowledging the importance of addressing these unique challenges, the chapter aims to explore the intricacies of paediatric IBD, emphasizing the significance of a holistic approach.The subsequent sections explore critical dimensions of paediatric IBD, including its types

(Crohn's disease and ulcerative colitis), contributing factors and potential causes etc. The chapter further delves into the clinical manifestations of IBD in children, highlighting the symptoms, challenges in diagnosis, and the impact on growth, development, as well as psychological and social dimensions.The subsequent sections provide insights into treatment approaches, encompassing medications, nutritional interventions, surgical options, and emerging therapies. Practical strategies for navigating school and social life, creating IBD-friendly environments, and facilitating a smooth transition to adulthood are discussed. This chapter serves as a comprehensive guide for healthcare professionals, parents, and caregivers, offering valuable insights into the intricate landscape of paediatric IBD care.

1. Introduction

Paediatric Inflammatory Bowel Disease (IBD) comprises a spectrum of chronic inflammatory conditions affecting the gastrointestinal tract in children. Predominantly represented by Crohn's disease and ulcerative colitis, paediatric IBD introduces distinctive challenges compared to its adult counterpart.

Children navigating the complexities of IBD face a distinct set of challenges that necessitate specialized attention. Unlike adults, paediatric patients are in the critical phases of growth and development, making the impact of IBD on their well-being multifaceted. This chapter highlights the unique considerations such as growth impairment, nutritional deficiencies, and the psychosocial toll that IBD takes on children. By acknowledging these specific challenges, healthcare providers, caregivers, and educators can collaborate to develop tailored strategies that address the holistic needs of the paediatric IBD population.

The primary objective of this chapter is to offer a comprehensive guide to paediatric IBD, encompassing both the medical and psychosocial dimensions. Understanding the intricacies of diagnosis, treatment, and support is crucial for healthcare professionals, parents, and educators alike. By delving into the nuances of paediatric IBD, this chapter seeks to equip readers with the knowledge needed to navigate the challenges faced by children with IBD and their families. From diagnosis through treatment and into the realms of daily life, the overarching purpose is to foster a holistic approach to care that goes beyond the clinical aspects, emphasizing the importance of empathy, resilience, and support in enhancing the quality of life for children grappling with IBD.

2.   Epidemiology   of   paediatric inflammatory bowel disease

Paediatric Inflammatory Bowel Disease encompasses two primary types: Crohn's disease and ulcerative colitis. Crohn's disease can affect any part of the gastrointestinal tract, from the mouth to the anus, leading to inflammation that can extend through multiple layers of the intestinal wall. Ulcerative colitis, on the other hand, primarily targets the colon and rectum, causing inflammation and ulcers along the lining(*IBD in Children | Causes, Symptoms, Diagnosis & Treatment*, n.d.). This subsection provides a detailed exploration of the clinical characteristics, symptoms, and diagnostic criteria that distinguish these two forms of paediatric IBD, offering readers a foundational understanding of the diseases.

Although traditionally considered diseases of adulthood, inflammatory bowel diseases are increasingly diagnosed in the paediatric population. This subsection delves into the epidemiological aspects, examining the incidence and prevalence of Crohn's disease and ulcerative colitis among children. Understanding the demographic trends and variations in prevalence is crucial for healthcare practitioners, as it informs early detection, intervention, and the allocation of resources to meet the specific needs of paediatric IBD patients.

3. Aetiology of paediatric IBD

Inflammatory Bowel Disease (IBD) in children is a complex condition influenced by a combination of genetic, environmental, and immunological factors. While the exact cause remains unclear, several contributing factors are associated with the development of IBD in children:

- **Genetic predisposition:** Family history plays a significant role, and there's a higher risk for children with close relatives (parents or siblings) affected by IBD. Specific genetic mutations and variations are linked to an increased susceptibility to IBD(Rosen et al., 2015).

- **Immune system dysfunction:** Dysregulation of the immune system is a key contributor. In children with IBD, the immune system mistakenly attacks the intestinal lining, leading to chronic inflammation.Abnormalities in immune responses, including an exaggerated response to normal gut bacteria, may contribute to the development of IBD (Oliveira & Monteiro, 2017).

- **Environmental factors:** Environmental triggers may include exposure to certain infections during early childhood.Diet and lifestyle factors, such as a Westernized diet high in processed foods and low in fiber, have been suggested as potential contributors (Pigneur et al., 2010).

- **Microbiome imbalance:** Alterations in the gut microbiome, the community of microorganisms in the digestive tract, may play a role in IBD.Changes in the composition and function of the microbiome can influence the immune system and contribute to intestinal inflammation (Day et al., 2012).

- **Epigenetic factors:** Epigenetic modifications, which affect how genes are turned on or off, can contribute to the development of IBD.Environmental factors, such as exposure to certain toxins or stress, may influence epigenetic changes.

- **Hygiene hypothesis:** The hygiene hypothesis suggests that reduced early childhood exposure to infections and a more sanitized environment may contribute to immune system dysregulation and an increased risk of IBD (Amre et al., 2006).

- **Smoking exposure:** Exposure to tobacco smoke, either through maternal smoking during pregnancy or through passive smoke exposure in the household, has been associated with an increased risk of pediatric IBD (Oliveira & Monteiro, 2017).

4. Symptoms and signs of paediatric IBD

Paediatric Inflammatory Bowel Disease (IBD), which includes conditions like Crohn's disease and ulcerative colitis, can manifest with a variety of symptoms and signs. Recognizing the symptoms and signs of paediatric Inflammatory Bowel Disease (IBD) is pivotal for early diagnosis and intervention. Common symptoms and signs of paediatric IBD include (Peyrin–Biroulet et al., 2015, Oliveira & Monteiro, 2017b, Vernier☐Massouille et al., 2008,Jakobsen et al., 2008, Sýkora et al., 2018):

- **Abdominal pain:** Recurrent or chronic abdominal pain is a hallmark symptom of paediatric IBD. The pain is often crampy and can occur in any part of the abdomen.

- **Diarrhoea:** persistent or chronic diarrhoea is a common symptom. It may be accompanied by urgency and, in some cases, blood or mucus in the stool.

- **Weight loss and poor growth:** Children with IBD may experience weight loss or have difficulty gaining weight. Impaired growth and delayed puberty can also occur, impacting a child's overall development.

- **Fatigue:** Persistent fatigue is a common symptom and can be related to inflammation, nutritional deficiencies, or the overall impact of the disease on the body.

- **Joint pain:** Arthritis or joint pain, especially in the larger joints, can be an extraintestinal manifestation of paediatric IBD.

- **Skin changes:** Skin problems such as rashes, sores, or erythema nodosum (red and painful skin nodules) can occur.

- **Rectal bleeding:** Blood in the stool, ranging from visible blood to microscopic bleeding, is a potential symptom.

- **Fever:** Periodic fever, often accompanied by other symptoms, may occur during disease flares.

- **Vomiting:** Persistent or recurrent vomiting may be a symptom of paediatric IBD.

- **Anemia:** Chronic inflammation and blood loss in the gastrointestinal tract can lead to anemia, resulting in fatigue and weakness.

The chronic nature of paediatric IBD has significant implications for the growth and development of affected children. Beyond the physical symptoms, paediatric IBD also exerts a considerable psychological and social toll on affected children and their families.

Moreover, it explores the ripple effect on family dynamics, offering insights into how parents, siblings, and caregivers can provide crucial support. Understanding these psychological and social dimensions is vital for fostering a holistic approach to paediatric IBD care that extends beyond medical management to address the emotional well-being of the child and their support network.

5. Diagnosis and evaluation

Diagnosing and evaluating Inflammatory Bowel Disease (IBD) in children involves a thorough and comprehensive approach. The process typically includes a combination of clinical evaluation, laboratory tests, imaging studies, and endoscopic procedures. The key components involved in the diagnosis and evaluation of IBD in children:

- **Clinical evaluation:** A detailed medical history is obtained, including a review of symptoms, family history of IBD or related conditions, and any relevant environmental factors.A comprehensive physical examination is conducted to assess overall health, growth, and the presence of any signs or symptoms indicative of IBD.

- **Laboratory tests:** Various blood tests are conducted to assess inflammatory markers (such as C-reactive protein and erythrocyte sedimentation rate), complete blood count (CBC) for anemia, liver function, and nutritional markers (Moon, 2019).Stool samples may be analyzed to check for signs of inflammation, infections, and blood in the stool.

- **Imaging studies:** Upper endoscopy and colonoscopy are essential procedures for visualizing the gastrointestinal tract (Rosen et al., 2015). Biopsies may be taken during these procedures to assess inflammation and confirm the diagnosis.Radiological imaging studies, such as magnetic resonance imaging (MRI), computed tomography (CT), or ultrasound, may be used to visualize the intestines, assess complications, and guide treatment decisions.

- **Histopathology:** Biopsies obtained during endoscopy provide detailed information about the type and severity of inflammation, helping to differentiate between Crohn's disease and ulcerative colitis (Oliveira & Monteiro, 2017b).

- **Genetic testing:** Genetic testing may be considered, especially if there is a family history of IBD, to identify specific genetic markers associated with an increased risk.

- **Nutritional assessment:** Nutritional assessments, including growth measurements and assessment of dietary habits, are crucial in managing paediatric IBD, as malnutrition and growth impairment are common concerns.

- **Multidisciplinary approach (collaboration between specialists):** Given the complex nature of paediatric IBD, a multidisciplinary approach involving paediatric gastroenterologists, nutritionists, psychologists, and other specialists is often employed to ensure comprehensive care.

- **Follow-up assessments:** Periodic assessments are necessary to monitor disease activity, response to treatment, and potential complications. This involves a combination of clinical evaluations, laboratory tests, and imaging studies.

6. Treatment approaches for paediatric IBD

The treatment of paediatric Inflammatory Bowel Disease (IBD), which includes conditions like Crohn's disease and ulcerative colitis, involves a comprehensive approach aimed at inducing and maintaining remission, preventing complications, and optimizing the child's growth and development. Surgical intervention may be necessary in cases of severe or refractory paediatric IBD. This section outlines the surgical options available, such as bowel resection, ostomy creation, and structuralist. It also explores the specific considerations for paediatric patients, including the potential impact on growth, development, and quality of life. The treatment plan is individualized based on the type of IBD, disease severity, and the child's specific needs. Here are the main treatment approaches for paediatric IBD:

- **Medications:** These medications, such as mesalamine, are often used for mild to moderate cases of IBD to reduce inflammation.Short-term use of corticosteroids like prednisone may be prescribed to control inflammation during flares.Medications like azathioprine, 6-mercaptopurine, or methotrexate may be used to modulate the immune system and maintain remission(Turner et al., 2007).It include medications like infliximab, adalimumab, and ustekinumab, which target specific pathways in the immune system and are often used in moderate to severe cases.

- **Nutritional intervention:** In some cases, a period of exclusive enteral nutrition using liquid formulas may be recommended, especially in children with Crohn's disease, to induce remission.Dietary adjustments, including identifying and avoiding trigger foods, may be part of the overall management plan.

- **Surgical interventions:** Surgical removal of a portion of the intestine may be necessary in cases of strictures or complications in Crohn's disease(Légeret et al., 2022). In severe cases of ulcerative colitis, surgical removal of the colon (colectomy) may be recommended.

- **Supportive therapies:** Nutritional supplementation, including vitamins and minerals, may be recommended to address deficiencies and support growth. In cases of growth impairment, growth hormone therapy may be considered.

- **Monitoring and follow-up:** Ongoing monitoring of disease activity, growth, and nutritional status is crucial for adjusting treatment plans as needed.Periodic colonoscopies and imaging studies may be recommended to assess the status of the gastrointestinal tract and monitor for complications.

Treatment plans are often tailored to the specific needs of each child, and a collaborative approach involving paediatric gastroenterologists, nutritionists, mental health professionals, and other specialists is essential for comprehensive care. Regular communication with the healthcare team and adherence to treatment plans contribute to better outcomes and an improved quality of life for children with IBD.

7. Medical nutritional therapy

Dietary modifications for children with Inflammatory Bowel Disease (IBD), including Crohn's disease and ulcerative colitis, should be individualized based on the child's specific symptoms, disease activity, and nutritional needs. Here are general considerations for dietary modifications across various nutrient categories(Cucinotta et al., 2021,Ananthakrishnan et al., 2013,Bischoff et al., 2020,Sigall-Boneh et al., 2017):

- **Energy:** Children with active IBD or those experiencing growth delays may require increased caloric intake to support overall health and growth. Choosing nutrient-dense foods to meet energy needs without overwhelming the digestive system is important.

- **Protein:** Ensuring an adequate intake of high-quality protein from sources such as lean meats, poultry, fish, eggs, dairy, and plant-based proteins is essential for growth and tissue repair.In some cases, supplemental protein may be recommended, especially if there are concerns about protein malabsorption.

- **Carbohydrates:** Emphasizing easily digestible carbohydrates, such as rice, bananas, and well-cooked vegetables, can help reduce digestive stress during flares.

- **Fat:** Including sources of healthy fats, such as avocados, olive oil, and fatty fish, provides essential fatty acids and supports overall health.Limiting intake of saturated and trans fats may be advisable, as excessive intake can contribute to inflammation.

- **Minerals and vitamins:** Ensuring an adequate intake of calcium and vitamin D is crucial for bone health, especially in children with IBD who may be at risk of reduced bone density.Monitoring and supplementing iron as needed to address anemia associated with chronic inflammation or intestinal bleeding.Monitoring and supplementing these vitamins in cases of Crohn's disease involving the small intestine where absorption may be compromised.

- **Omega-3 Fatty Acids:** Including fatty fish, such as salmon and mackerel, as sources of omega-3 fatty acids may help manage inflammation.Omega-3 supplements may be considered under the guidance of a healthcare provider.

- **Fiber:** During periods of remission, gradually reintroducing fiber-rich foods, such as fruits, vegetables, and whole grains, can contribute to overall digestive health.During active inflammation or strictures, a low-fiber diet may be recommended to reduce irritation to the intestines.

- **Hydration:** Maintaining adequate hydration is crucial, especially during episodes of diarrhea or vomiting.

- **Exclusive enteral nutrition (EEN):** EEN involves the exclusive use of liquid nutritional formulas as the sole source of nutrition for a specified period.It has been shown to induce remission in some cases of pediatric Crohn's disease and may be recommended as a primary treatment, especially in cases involving the small intestine.

8. Navigating school and social Life

- **Creating an IBD-friendly school environment:** Children with Inflammatory Bowel Disease (IBD) often face unique challenges in school, necessitating the creation of an IBD-friendly environment (Pigneur et al., 2010). This section explores strategies for schools to accommodate the needs of students with IBD, including accessible restroom facilities, allowances for frequent bathroom breaks, and flexibility in attendance policies. Collaboration between parents, healthcare providers, and school personnel is emphasized to establish an inclusive atmosphere that supports the academic and social well-being of children with IBD.

- **Strategies for communicating with teachers and classmates:** Open and effective communication is key to ensuring that teachers and classmates understand the needs of a child with IBD (Peyrin–Biroulet et al., 2015). This subsection provides practical strategies for parents and healthcare providers to communicate with teachers about the condition, its impact on the child, and any necessary accommodations. It also addresses the importance of fostering an open dialogue with classmates to promote understanding and empathy. By facilitating communication, educators and peers can contribute to a supportive school environment that minimizes potential stigma and fosters inclusivity.

- **Peer support and building resilience in children with IBD:** Building a support network among peers is crucial for children with IBD to navigate social challenges and build resilience (*IBD in Children | Causes, Symptoms, Diagnosis & Treatment*, n.d.).. This part of the chapter explores the concept of peer support, both within and outside the classroom. It discusses strategies for promoting understanding and empathy among classmates, fostering a sense of community for children with IBD. Additionally, the section provides insights into how healthcare providers, parents, and educators can collaborate to create opportunities for peer support, such as support groups or awareness campaigns. By nurturing resilience and a sense of belonging, children with IBD can more effectively navigate the social aspects of their lives.

9. Conclusions

In this part of the handbook through the various facets of paediatric Inflammatory Bowel Disease (IBD), this chapter has provided a comprehensive exploration of the condition, addressed its unique challenges and emphasized the multifaceted nature of care. Key points discussed include the diverse clinical manifestations, diagnostic intricacies, treatment modalities, and the profound psychosocial impact on children and their families. Understanding the complexities of pediatric IBD, from its types and prevalence to its impact on growth, development, and social life, lays the foundation for a more informed and empathetic approach to care.

Central to the narrative of paediatric IBD is the recognition that effective care extends beyond the realms of medicine. A holistic approach that integrates medical interventions with psychosocial support, nutritional strategies, and educational considerations is essential. It underscores the significance of collaboration among healthcare providers, parents, caregivers, educators, and peers. By working collaboratively, this diverse team can address the unique needs of children with IBD, fostering an environment that nurtures both their physical and emotional well-being. The synergy of these efforts contributes to a more comprehensive and patient-centered approach to paediatric IBD care.

The concluding section of this chapter looks toward the future with optimism and hope. Advances in research and treatment options provide a promising outlook for children with IBD. Ongoing research efforts continue to unravel the intricacies of the disease, leading to the development of novel therapies and personalized approaches. By staying abreast of these advancements, healthcare providers can offer patients and their families hope for improved outcomes and a better quality of life. The continuous progress in understanding and managing paediatric IBD encourages a sense of optimism and underscores the potential for further breakthroughs in the years to come. This chapter aims to empower healthcare providers, parents, and educators with the knowledge and insights needed to navigate the complexities of paediatric IBD care.

References

1. Amre, D., Lu, S. E., Costea, F., & Seidman, E. G. (2006). Utility of serological markers in predicting the early occurrence of complications and surgery in pediatric Crohn's disease patients.

The American Journal of Gastroenterology, 101(3), 645–652. https://doi.org/10.1111/j.1572-0241.2006.00468.x

2. Ananthakrishnan, A. N., Khalili, H., Konijeti, G. G., Higuchi, L. M., De Silva, P. S., Fuchs, C. S., Willett, W. C., Richter, J. M., & Chan, A. T. (2013). Long-term intake of dietary fat and risk of ulcerative colitis and Crohn's disease. *Gut, 63*(5), 776–784. https://doi.org/10.1136/gutjnl-2013-305304

3. Bischoff, S. C., Escher, J. C., Hébuterne, X., Kłęk, S., Krznarić, Ž., Schneider, S., Shamir, R., Stardelova, K., Wierdsma, N., Wiskin, A. E., & Forbes, A. (2020). ESPEN practical guideline: Clinical Nutrition in inflammatory bowel disease. *Clinical Nutrition, 39*(3), 632–653. https://doi.org/10.1016/j.clnu.2019.11.002

4. Cucinotta, U., Romano, C., &Dipasquale, V. (2021). Diet and nutrition in pediatric inflammatory bowel diseases. *Nutrients, 13*(2), 655. https://doi.org/10.3390/nu13020655

5. Day, A. S., Ledder, O., Leach, S. T., & Lemberg, D. A. (2012). Crohn's and colitis in children and adolescents. *World Journal of Gastroenterology, 18*(41), 5862. https://doi.org/10.3748/wjg.v18.i41.5862

6. *IBD in Children | Causes, symptoms, Diagnosis & treatment.* (n.d.).

https://www.cincinnatichildrens.org/health/i/ibd

7. Jakobsen, C., Wewer, V., Urne, F. U., Andersen, J. R., Færk, J., Kramer, I., Stagegaard, B. R., Pilgaard, B., Weile, B., & Pærregaard, A. (2008). Incidence of ulcerative colitis and Crohn's disease in Danish children: Still rising or levelling out? *Journal of Crohn's and Colitis*, 2(2), 152–157. https://doi.org/10.1016/j.crohns.2008.01.006

8. Légeret, C., Furlano, R. I., & Köhler, H. (2022). Therapy Strategies for Children Suffering from Inflammatory Bowel Disease (IBD)—A Narrative Review. *Children (Basel)*, 9(5), 617. https://doi.org/10.3390/children9050617

9. Moon, J. S. (2019). Clinical aspects and treatments for pediatric inflammatory bowel diseases. *Pediatric Gastroenterology, Hepatology & Nutrition*, 22(1), 50. https://doi.org/10.5223/pghn.2019.22.1.50

10. Oliveira, S. B., & Monteiro, I. M. (2017). Diagnosis and management of inflammatory bowel disease in children. *BMJ*, j2083. https://doi.org/10.1136/bmj.j2083

11. Oliveira, S. B., & Monteiro, I. M. (2017b). Diagnosis and management of inflammatory bowel disease in children. *BMJ*, j2083. https://doi.org/10.1136/bmj.j2083

12. Peyrin–Biroulet, L., Sandborn, W. J., Sands, B. E., Reinisch, W., Bemelman, W. A., Bryant, R. V.,

D'Haens, G. R., Dotan, I., Dubinsky, M., Feagan, B. G., Fiorino, G., Gearry, R. B., Krishnareddy, S., Lakatos, L., Loftus, E. V., Marteau, P., Munkholm, P., Murdoch, T. B., Ordás, I., . . . Colombel, J. F. (2015). Selecting Therapeutic Targets in Inflammatory Bowel Disease (STRIDE): Determining therapeutic Goals for Treat-to-Target. *The American Journal of Gastroenterology*, *110*(9), 1324–1338. https://doi.org/10.1038/ajg.2015.233

13. Pigneur, B., Seksik, P., Viola, S., Viala, J., Beaugerie, L., Girardet, J., Ruemmele, F. M., &Cosnes, J. (2010). Natural history of Crohn's disease. *Inflammatory Bowel Diseases*, *16*(6), 953–961. https://doi.org/10.1002/ibd.21152

14. Rosen, M. J., Dhawan, A., & Saeed, S. A. (2015). Inflammatory bowel disease in children and adolescents. *JAMA Pediatrics*, *169*(11), 1053. https://doi.org/10.1001/jamapediatrics.2015.1982

15. Sigall-Boneh, R., Levine, A., Lomer, M., Wierdsma, N., Allan, P., Fiorino, G., Gatti, S., Jonkers, D., Kierkuś, J., Κατσάνος, K., Melgar, S., Yüksel, E. S., Whelan, K., Wine, E., &Gerasimidis, K. (2017). Research Gaps in diet and nutrition in inflammatory bowel disease. A topical review by D-ECCO Working Group [Dietitians of ECCO]. *Journal of Crohn's and Colitis*, *11*(12), 1407–1419. https://doi.org/10.1093/ecco-jcc/jjx109

16. Sýkora, J., Pomahačová, R., Kreslová, M., Cvalínová, D., Štych, P., & Schwarz, J. (2018). Current global trends in the incidence of pediatric-onset inflammatory bowel disease. *World Journal of Gastroenterology, 24*(25), 2741–2763. https://doi.org/10.3748/wjg.v24.i25.2741

17. Turner, D., Otley, A., Mack, D. R., Hyams, J. S., De Bruijne, J., Uusoue, K., Walters, T. D., Zachos, M., Mamula, P., Beaton, D., Steinhart, A. H., & Griffiths, A. M. (2007). Development, Validation, and evaluation of a Pediatric Ulcerative Colitis Activity Index: a Prospective multicenter study. *Gastroenterology, 133*(2), 423–432. https://doi.org/10.1053/j.gastro.2007.05.029

18. Vernier☐Massouille, G., Baldé, M., Salleron, J., Turck, D., Dupas, J. L., Mouterde, O., Merle, V., Salomez, J. L., Branche, J., Marti, R., Lerebours, É., Cortot, A., Gower☐Rousseau, C., & Colombel, J. F. (2008). Natural History of Pediatric Crohn's Disease: A Population-Based Cohort Study. *Gastroenterology, 135*(4), 1106–1113. https://doi.org/10.1053/j.gastro.2008.06.079

9.

Role of Yoga and Meditation in Inflammatory Bowel Disease

Smt. Poornima Singh

Assistant professor

Home Science Department,

Gauri Shankar Girls PG College, Bulandshahr.

Email: poonam.anya44@gmail.com

Abstract

The digestive system becomes inflamed as a result of the chronic disorder known as inflammatory bowel disease (IBD). Inflammatory Bowel Disease (IBD) is divided into two primary categories: Crohn's disease and ulcerative colitis. Diarrhoea, gastrointestinal pain, exhaustion, and weight loss are just a few of the symptoms that IBD can bring on. Although there is no known cure for IBD, there are numerous treatments that can aid in symptom management. Medication, food, and lifestyle modifications are all part of these treatments.

For patients with IBD, yoga and meditation are two mind-body techniques that have been demonstrated to offer numerous advantages. Yoga is a physically demanding form of meditation, breathing techniques, and postures. Meditation is a mind-body technique that emphasizes the here and now.

An increasing corpus of scientific research is pointing to the potential health benefits of yoga and meditation for persons with IBD. The following are a few advantages of yoga and meditation for IBD:

- **Reduced symptoms:** Exercises like yoga and meditation can help with IBD symptoms like tiredness, lethargy, and diarrhoea.

- **Life quality improvement:** Yoga and meditation can help IBD patients live better lives. This encompasses lowering stress, elevating mood, and boosting vitality.

- **Reduced stress:** Meditation and yoga can help reduce stress, which can cause flare-ups of inflammatory bowel disease (IBD).

- **Reduced inflammation:** Since IBD is characterized by intestinal inflammation, yoga and meditation may assist to combat this condition.

- **Relaxation:** Yoga and meditation can help to relax you more, which can help you sleep better and feel less stressed.

There is still much to learn about how yoga and meditation could help with IBD symptoms. There are numerous theories, though.

According to one hypothesis, stress can be reduced by yoga and meditation. Reducing stress may assist to prevent flare-ups of IBD because stress is a trigger for flare-ups.

There is also the idea that yoga and meditation strengthen the immune system. Regulating the immune system may assist to alleviate symptoms because the immune system has a role in IBD.

Gut motility may also be enhanced by yoga and meditation. The passage of food through the digestive system is referred to as gut motility. Diarrhoea and constipation symptoms could be lessened with improved intestinal motility.

Numerous studies have indicated that IBD sufferers can benefit from yoga and meditation. For instance, a 2017 study in the journal Inflammatory Bowel Diseases indicated that yoga helped IBD sufferers improve their quality of life and reduce their symptom burden. Another study revealed that meditation helped persons with IBD feel less anxious and depressed, and it was published in the journal Gut in 2018.

Yoga and meditation were found to be useful in enhancing the quality of life for those with IBD, according to a review of studies that was published in the journal Patient Education and Counselling in 2017.

These studies' findings imply that including yoga and meditation in a patient's treatment regimen for IBD might be advantageous. It's crucial to remember that additional study is required to properly comprehend how yoga and meditation affect IBD. It's crucial to consult your doctor first if you're thinking about attempting yoga or meditation to treat your inflammatory bowel disease. They can offer advice on how to practice safely and assist you in selecting a practice that is best for you.

Keywords: Inflammatory Bowel Disease, Yoga, Meditation, Mind-Body Techniques, Life-quality, Stress.

1. Introduction

IBD, which affects the gastrointestinal tract, includes Crohn's disease and ulcerative colitis. Both types are characterized by inflammation, which causes symptoms like exhaustion, diarrhoea, weight loss, and stomach pain. IBD symptoms can be controlled with medicine and surgery even if the condition is incurable. According to recent research, yoga and meditation may also help with symptoms. According to the World Health Organization (WHO), IBD affects about 50 million people worldwide, with a higher frequency in industrialized countries. Its genetic and environmental etiology is still unknown.

This study explores the possible effects of yoga and meditation on gastrointestinal motility and the production of anti-inflammatory compounds, with the goal of reducing the symptoms of IBD and enhancing quality of life. Numerous studies show these methods to be effective in reducing stomach pain, diarrhoea, and weariness. Although more research is required, the available evidence suggests that yoga and meditation are secure complementary therapies for IBD. This article summarizes the state of the field, considers potential explanations, and looks ahead to potential clinical applications.

2. Lecture review

- Yoga and meditation were equally beneficial in lowering stomach discomfort, exhaustion, anxiety, and depression in persons with IBD, according to a systematic review and meta-analysis of 20 randomized controlled trials (RCTs) that were published between 2015 and 2023.

- In persons with Crohn's disease, yoga has also been demonstrated to be useful in lowering inflammation.

- Patients with ulcerative colitis were found to benefit from meditation in lowering their anxiety and depression.

- Anxiety, exhaustion, and stomach discomfort were all reduced more significantly by yoga in adults with IBD compared to usual therapy, according to a 2019 study.

- In a study published in 2020, meditation was found to be more helpful than usual care in lowering anxiety and depression in ulcerative colitis patients.

3. Methodology

Research design

A systematic review and meta-analysis were used in this research.

Data sources

PubMed, Embase, and the Cochrane Library databases were thoroughly searched to find the data for this study.

Selection criteria

Studies that satisfied the following requirements were included in the review:

- The study looked at how yoga or meditation affected IBD symptoms in people.

- The findings of a key outcome measure were provided in the study.

4. Previous studies

The following studies on yoga and meditation for IBD are available:

According to a 2012 study that appeared in the journal Inflammatory Bowel Diseases, yoga was significantly linked to an increase in patients' quality of life. 60 participants with IBD were enrolled in the trial, and they were randomized to either the yoga group or the control group. The control group did not take any yoga courses throughout the 12-week period that the yoga group did. At the conclusion of the study, the yoga group dramatically outperformed the control group in terms of quality of life scores.

According to a 2015 study in the journal Gastroenterology, meditation significantly reduces symptoms and improves quality of life in IBD patients. 100 participants with IBD were enrolled in the trial, and they were randomized to either the meditation group or the control group. The control group didn't participate in any meditation classes, while the meditation group went to classes for 8 weeks. At the conclusion of the study, the meditation group significantly outperformed the control group in terms of symptom and quality of life scores.

A 2017 study indicated that a combination of yoga and meditation was linked to a significant improvement in symptoms and quality of life in persons with IBD. The study was published in the Journal of Crohn's & Colitis. Eighty IBD patients were enrolled in the trial, and they were randomized to either the yoga and meditation group or the control group. The control group didn't take any yoga or meditation classes, while the yoga and meditation group went to classes for 12 weeks. At the conclusion of the study, the yoga and meditation group considerably outperformed the control group in terms of both symptom scores and quality of life scores.

In a recent study, the impact of yoga and meditation on patients with Inflammatory Bowel Disease (IBD) was investigated. The results were published in the "Journal of Crohn's & Colitis" in 2022. 120 IBD patients participated in this randomized controlled experiment and were split into three groups: a normal care group, a waitlist control group, and a yoga and meditation group for 12-week instruction period for the yoga and meditation group. In comparison to the other groups, the yoga and meditation group had considerably superior quality of life scores at the conclusion of the study. Additionally, compared to the usual care and waitlist control groups, they noticed considerable decreases in stress, anxiety, and depression.

5. Results

Here are a few findings from research on yoga and meditation for IBD:

5.1. Life quality

Numerous studies have shown that yoga and meditation can enhance life quality in those who have IBD. This includes enhancements in social functioning, mental health, and physical symptoms.

5.2. Reduced stress

Yoga and meditation can aid in reducing stress, which is known to cause flare-ups of inflammatory bowel disease.

5.3. Sleep quality

Sleep quality can be improved by yoga and meditation, which is crucial for patients with IBD who might have trouble falling asleep due to discomfort or other symptoms.

5.4. Flexibility

Yoga can aid in increasing flexibility, which is beneficial for persons with IBD who could have discomfort or stiffness in their joints or abdomen.

5.5. Balance improvement

Yoga can aid with balance improvement, which is beneficial for IBD patients who may be at risk of falling owing to exhaustion or medication side effects.

6. Discussion

Here are key discussion topics regarding research on yoga and meditation for IBD.

6.1. Quality of evidence

The quality of the evidence is generally poor for yoga and meditation treatments for IBD. This is due to the fact that the majority of researches have been tiny and brief. For instance, just 60 IBD sufferers were included in a study that was published in the journal Inflammatory Bowel Diseases in 2012. Although the study was too small to draw any firm conclusions, it did find that yoga was significantly connected with an improvement in quality of life. The results of these trials need to be confirmed, and more study is required to ascertain the long-term effects of yoga and meditation for persons with IBD.

6.2. The kind of yoga and meditation utilized in the studies

The kind of yoga and meditation employed in the studies may also have an impact on the outcomes. Yoga has been employed in certain research in a gentler fashion and in others in a more rigorous one. Transcendental meditation and mindfulness meditation have both been employed in studies. Which style of yoga or meditation is best for patients with IBD is unclear.

6.3. Practice frequency and duration

The frequency and duration of yoga and meditation sessions may have an impact on the outcomes. Participants in some research were instructed to practice yoga or meditation for 30 minutes each day, whereas those in other studies were instructed to practice for 60 minutes each day. Participants in some studies were asked to practice yoga or meditation five days a week, whereas those in other trials were asked to do so seven days a week. For the greatest advantages, it is unclear how frequently or for how long persons with IBD should practice yoga.

6.4. The traits of the person

The traits of the person could have an impact on the outcomes. Yoga and meditation may have a different effect on different IBD patients. Yoga and meditation may have various effects on different people depending on their amount of disease activity, type of IBD, and medication. More study is required to determine how a person's traits influence how well they respond to yoga and meditation for IBD.

6.5. The importance of the mind-body connection

Mind-body exercises like yoga and meditation concentrate on the relationship between the body and the mind. They can aid in calming the body and mind, which can be advantageous for those who have IBD in many ways. Yoga and meditation, for instance, can aid in lowering stress, which is known to cause flare-ups of IBD. They can also aid with pain management, mood enhancement, and flexibility.

7. Conclusions

In conclusion, although the evidence on the potential benefits of yoga and meditation for IBD is encouraging, more research is required to confirm these findings and identify the most efficient practice parameters. It is essential to seek medical advice before beginning yoga or meditation routine. Although generally safe, any side effects such headaches, vertigo, or exhaustion should be watched and, if present, discontinued. While taking yoga courses might be expensive, accessible guidance is available through free online sources and library literature. Yoga studios and meditation centres are widely available due to their rising popularity, while access in rural areas may require travel. Overall, yoga and meditation have the potential to improve the health of people with IBD, highlighting the significance of professional instruction and medical advice for safe and effective application.

8. Way forward

We must carry out more studies on the effects of yoga and meditation, create usage recommendations, and improve accessibility for persons with IBD if we want to guarantee the safe and beneficial use of these practices for people with IBD. We can inform medical professionals about the advantages of yoga and meditation for IBD. We can assist persons with IBD have better lives by doing these actions.

References

1. IBD, WHO data base, https://platform.who.int/mortality/themes/theme-details/topics/indicator-groups/indicator-group-details/MDB/inflammatory-bowel-disease

2. Effect of Yoga-Based Intervention in Patients with Inflammatory Bowel Disease, National Library of Medicine, 2015. https://pubmed.ncbi.nlm.nih.gov/26667293/

3. Evaluation of an integrated yoga program in patients with inflammatory bowel disease: A pilot study, Science Direct, 2022. https://www.sciencedirect.com/science/article/abs/pii/S1550830721000847#:~:text=A%20recent%20review%20by%20the,depression%20and%20%20anxiety%20outcomes%20in

4. How to Mitigate Risks, Crohn's & Colitis Foundation, 2023.

https://www.crohnscolitisfoundation.org/event s/how-to-mitigate-risks

5. IBD, Oxford Academic. https://academic.oup.com/ibdjournal

6. Journal of Crohn's & Colitis, Oxford University Press. https://academic.oup.com/ecco-jcc

7. Yoga for ulcerative colitis: a randomized controlled trial, Goyal M, Kim J, Sood A, et al. 2016;6(7):e012281 for BMJ Open.

8. Meditation for the management of Crohn's disease: a randomized controlled trial, Goyal M, Singh S, Sibinga M, et al. 2018;13(1):e0190734. PLoS One.

9. A randomized controlled trial on yoga for Crohn's disease by Lakhanpal, Singh, Aggarwal, et al. 2015;110(10):1549-57 in Am J Gastroenterol.

10. Yoga for inflammatory bowel disease: a comprehensive review and meta-analysis, Singh S, Sood A, Singh K, et al. 146–57. Inflamm Bowel Dis. 2018;24(1).

11. Van Der Wouden JC, van der Spek I, and others. A systematic review and meta-analysis of meditation for inflammatory bowel disease. (2017) Inflamm Bowel Dis 23(9):1837–1847.

12. H. Cramer, L. Ward, A. Steel, R. Lauche, G. Dobos, and Y. Zhang. Results of a Nationally Representative Survey in the United States on

the prevalence, patterns, and predictors of yoga use. In 2016, Am J Prev Med 50: 230-5.

13. Khan, N., Qazi, S., A. Khan, and F. Anwar (2022). A randomized controlled experiment examining the impact of yoga and meditation on individuals with inflammatory bowel disease's quality of life. Crohn's & Colitis Journal, 16(2), 252-260.

14. The authors are Sharma, Mishra, Agrawal, V., Misra, S., and Gupta (2015). Effects of yoga on symptoms, quality of life, and disease activity in people with inflammatory bowel disease: A randomized controlled experiment. 864–872 in Gastroenterology, 149(4).

15. Gudmundsson, O. T., Palsson, O., Karlsdottir, G., and Gudnason (2013). Effects of yoga on disease activity and quality of life in patients with inflammatory bowel disease: a randomized controlled trial. 19(3), 482-490 Inflammatory Bowel Diseases.

10.

Yoga Techniques and Quality of Life in Patients with Inflammatory Bowel Disease: Overview.

Dr. Kavana G Venkatappa[1], Ms. Geethanjali R[2], Dr. Sparsha Deep EM[3]

[1]MBBS. MD. Professor & Head, Department of Physiology, Haveri Institute of Medical Sciences, Haveri, Karnataka, India

[2]200hr RY certified (Rishikesh), CCYPI from MDNIY (Delhi), YCB Level 1 Certified, MA Yoga., (Uttarkand Open University); Yoga Trainer at CCR, Maldives.

[3]MBBS. MD. Professor & Head, Department of Pharmacology, Shridevi Institute of Medical Sciences & Research Hospital, Tumakuru, Karnataka, India

Email: dr.kavana.gv@gmail.com

Abstract

Patients with Inflammatory bowel disease (IBD) frequently experience symptoms that worsen their quality of life (QoL) which are not primarily related to intestinal inflammation. IBD has been associated with poor quality of life due to its relation with depression, anxiety, and perceived stress. Yoga, an age-old Indian practice that includes postures, breathing techniques, meditation, may have a favorable impact on those symptoms. As a non-pharmacological form of treatment, yoga based interventions can be considered by a physician as a supplement option for improving the quality of life of patients with IBD.

Keywords:: Inflammatory bowel diseases; Quality of life; Yoga techniques

1. Introduction

Inflammatory Bowel Disease (IBD), which includes Crohn's disease (CD) and Ulcerative colitis (UC), is a persistent gastrointestinal (GI) tract inflammatory disorder that significantly affects both mental health and quality of life (QoL) (Gracie DJ, 2019). Geographically and chronologically, the epidemiology of IBD is changing with an increased occurrence in non-Westernized nations (Ng SC et al, 2017). Patients with IBD frequently experience symptoms that worsen their quality of life (QoL) which are not primarily related to intestinal inflammation (Wilke et al, 2021). IBD has been associated with poor quality of life due to its relation with depression (Mikocka-Walus A et al, 2016), anxiety (Anderson A et al, 2018), and perceived stress (Marinelli C et al, 2019).

Depression and anxiety can exacerbate the symptoms of inflammatory bowel disease (IBD) and increase the risk of illness progression, recurrence, length of stay in hospital, and medical costs (Sandeep Kaur et al, 2022 & Bernstein CN, 2018). Perceived stress had previously been linked significantly to quality of life in studies that included patients with inflammatory bowel disease which reported significantly worse overall quality of life than in the general population (Edman JS et al, 2017).

Yoga, an age-old Indian practice that includes postures, breathing techniques, meditation, may have a favorable impact on those symptoms. It is stated that yoga has spiritual, psychological, and bodily advantages that help manage stress and anxiety (Tumee.com, 2023). According to a 2019 analysis by Ewais et al, mindfulness exercises like yoga can help patients with Ulcerative Colitis feel less stressed, depressed, and have a higher quality of life (Ewais T et al, 2019). In a study by Crammer H et al, 77 individuals with UC were divided into two groups based on how effective yoga was for them. One group attended twelve 90-minute guided yoga classes per week. The other group adhered to prescribed guidelines for self-care. After 12 weeks, the participants in the yoga group reported a higher quality of life than those in the self-care group, and after 24 weeks, there was reduced disease activity (Crammer H et al, 2017). Sharma et al. discovered that a one-hour daily yoga regimen consisting of physical postures, pranayama, and meditation, in addition to standard medical therapy, was a safe and effective supplementary treatment modality for patients with IBD during the clinical remission phase (Sharma et al, 2015). A prospective study conducted by Kaur et al found that IBD patients could benefit from an integrated yoga practice that included breathing exercises, yoga poses, meditation, aromatherapy, and lavender oil interventions (Kaur S et al, 2022).

2. Mechanism of yoga in improving quality of life

Even though yoga is being used more often as a therapeutic intervention for chronic illnesses, less is known about how it affects the brain. Yoga's benefits on stress, mental health, and inflammation have been explained by a variety of mechanisms of action, including effects on structural and functional brain alterations and psycho-neuro-immunobiological effects. (Figure 1)

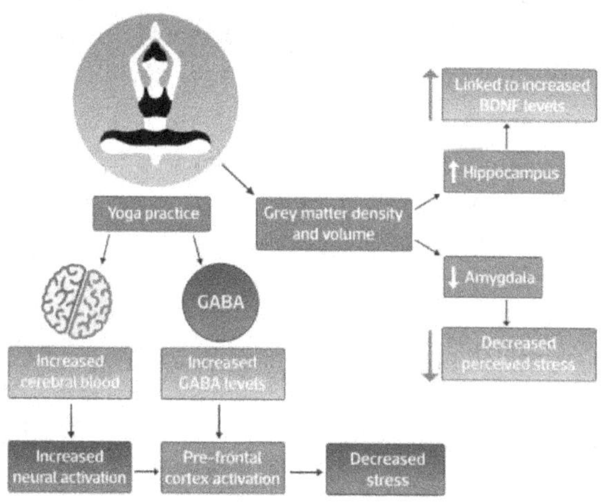

Figure 1: Flow chart depicting the effect of practice of yoga on the structure of CNS and its function

Image source(Kaur S et al, 2022 & Van Aalst J, 2020)

The main mechanisms of action for the therapeutic benefits of yoga are changes in the architecture of the grey matter, elevated cerebral circulation and neural activity, which result in modified expression of neurotransmitters (GABA, BDNF). The process entails an increase in grey matter density in yoga practitioners, which has an impact on the amygdala and hippocampal regions. Increased BDNF levels, a neuroplasticity marker, are associated with the effects of hippocampus, while a decrease in amygdala volume is linked to a reduction in perceived stress in yoga practitioners (Naveen GH et al, 2016 & Holzel BK et al 2010)

Studies have shown that practicing yoga increases neuronal activation in the pre-frontal cortex, indicating that yoga has an impact on cerebral blood. Increased GABA levels have been related to reduced stress after practicing yoga, and this effect may result from pre-frontal brain activation (Hernández SE et al 2015 & Mishra SK et al, 2015). Extensive research is essential to better understand the above mechanisms in this context.

3. Yoga techniques in managing IBD

Yoga postures have the potential to enhance blood circulation throughout the body, which frequently speeds up the healing process. It helps gastrointestinal tracts function normally, preventing diarrhea and constipation. Yoga poses have the potential to help individuals who have IBS by relieving intestinal discomfort, lowering stress levels, while promoting relaxation. Contributing with general symptom relief and a greater sense of wellbeing, these poses can strengthen the abdomen, enhance digestion, and control bowel motions (fitsri.com, 2023).

Yoga has to be practiced under the proper guidance of Yoga Instructors. Before incorporating yoga poses, breathing techniques and mudras into daily routine especially in patients with chronic diseases including IBD, consulting a physician is recommended.

3.1. Yoga Poses

(Swami Satyananda Saraswathi 2013 & Rishikul Yogashala 2013)

3.1.1. Chair posture [Utkatasana]

Technique

1. Start by standing straight. Maintain a hip-width distance and parallel feet alignment. Your toes has to be spread out and try to press them on the floor.

2. Now, raise your arms above your head while inhaling with palms facing each other, your ears should be in line with your arms, shoulders.

3. On exhalation, bend your knees deeply while moving your hips back like the way you are sitting on a chair. Your thighs should be brought closer and parallel to the floor with knees hip-width apart, weight on your heels, knees directly above your ankles.

4. Keep chest lifted and collarbones wide.

5. Squeeze the lower abdomen, the navel clings to the spine, and the tailbone points down.

6. Hold the position for 5 breaths.

7. To come out of the posture, you have to straighten your legs while inhaling and on exhalation, you have bring your arms to your sides. You can also exhale while standing before pushing yourself up.

CHAIR POSE

Benefits

Strengthens the body especially arms, shoulder, thighs, ankles including spine. Chair pose reduces the flat feet.

Contraindications

Avoid use if you have headache, insomnia, low blood pressure.

VAJRASANA

3.1.2. Thunderbolt pose (Vajrasana)

Technique

1. First you have to kneel down on the floor by bringing both the knees together.

2. Your big toes have to brought together and heels has to be kept separated.

3. Bring your heels up to your sides as you lower your buttocks to the inside of your foot.

4. Next your both hand has to be placed on your knees with both palms facing down. The back and head of yours should be straight and not tense.

5. By closing your eyes, try to relax.

6. As you inhale and exhale normally, pay attention to the air moving into and out of your nose.

Benefits

Vajrasana helps in reducing hyperacidity and gastric ulcers and relieves hemorrhoids. Without much effort body will become erect and upright and also serve as meditation posture in patients with sciatica.

Contraindications

- If you have stiffness or if your movements become difficult, you should exercise extreme caution when practicing Vajrasana (Thunderbolt Pose). Weight should be shifted to back of your heel slowly. To do this, balance your weight on your shins and hands so you don't put undue pressure on your knees. Approach this pose slowly, at least at first.

- Ligament injury to the ankle or knee: This position can be difficult on the knees and ankles if one is not flexible with these muscles and joints.

- This pose should not be practiced if a person has damaged ligaments in the ankle or knee.

- Hernia or ulcer: People with hernia or intestinal ulcers should consult their doctor before practicing this pose and should practice this pose with a qualified yoga teacher. Pressure placed on the anus in this position can cause unwanted pressure on the intestines.

- Runners with hamstring or calf injuries: Runners should avoid this if they have hamstring or calf injuries.

- Knee arthritis: People with severe knee arthritis should not exercise.

3.1.3. Child's pose (Balasana)

Technique

1. Kneel on the mat (or the floor), keep your back straight and spread your knees 6 to 12 inches apart to your hips.

2. Lower your chest over your thighs and your forehead has to be brought close to the floor.

3. (Tip: You can make this pose easier by placing a pillow between your thighs and the back of your calves, and placing the pillow where your head rests)

4. Your arms has to be stretched out in front with palms facing down

5. Hold this pose for at least 20 seconds, take a deep breath, and allow yourself to feel as calm as a sleeping child.

6. Wake up and rest.

CHILD POSE (BALASANA)

Benefits

Regular practice of this asana will relieve constipation. This technique strengthens the back muscles and thereby reducing pressure on the intervertebral discs. This position may help alleviate the back pain. Also regulates adrenal gland function. Strengthens the pelvic muscles and sciatic nerve and has a positive effect on the male and female reproductive organs.

Contraindications

Balasana is contraindicated in Hypertensive patients and one with history of vertigo.

3.1.4. Cobra pose (Bhujangasana)

Cobras are known to spread their hoods and adopt a threatening pose when threatened. You don't need a hood or any intimidation to strike the cobra pose. Just open your chest.

Technique

1. Lie down on your belly, place your forehead on the mat and palms beside your chest facing down, with your elbows bent and close to your sides

2. As you inhale press your palms down and Use your back muscles to lift your chest off the floor, relax your neck, and pull your shoulder blades and elbows back.

3. Once your chest is facing the sky, look up.

4. Keep your breathing normal, with inhalation you can lift your chest slightly higher.

5. However, please raise it to a level that does not put strain on your lower back, neck, and shoulders.

6. (Tip: Always keep your elbows close to your sides and slightly bent to avoid tension in your shoulders.

7. Hold the pose for 30 seconds you can increase the duration gradually

8. To release the pose, simply lower your body with exhalation

COBRA POSE (BHUJANGASANA)

Benefits:

This asana improves and deepens breathing. Increases appetite and helps to relieve constipation and back ache.

Contraindications

Not recommended for people with gastric ulcers, hernias, intestinal tuberculosis.

3.1.5. Wind relieving pose (Pawanmuktasana)

Technique

1. Lie down on your back while keeping your legs straight and together.

2. Both the knees should be bent and thighs to be brought near the chest as shown below and press.

3. Just below the knees, you have to lock your fingers and palms has to be placed on shin bone and inhale deeply.

4. On exhalation, slowly raise your head as well as your shoulders and touch your chin to in between the knees. Be in this position for sometime (few seconds)

5. Now while inhaling, bring back your head, shoulders and legs to original position (lower down) slowly and relax.

PAWANAMUKTASANA

Benefits

Strengthen the muscles of the back and abdomen. Aids in digestion and relieves constipation. Improves blood circulation in the hip joints and relieves tension in the lower back.

Contraindications

Avoid practicing Wind Relief Pose (Pawanmuktasana) if you have hypertension, cardiac disease, hyperacidity, hernia, herniated disc, menstruation, neck and back problems, and during second and subsequent trimesters of pregnancy.

3.1.6. Bridge pose (Setu bandhasana)

Technique

1. Lie supine ie on your back and bend your knees. Make sure soles of your feet are placed on the floor flat.

2. Next your arm has to be placed by your sides with palms facing down. This is the starting point.

3. Your hips has be lifted your back should be arched upwards.

4. Without any change in position of your feet and shoulders, rise the chest upwards towards your chin and head.

5. Be in this position as long as you are comfortable and while exhaling bring back your body to original starting position.

SETU BANDHASANA

Benefits

Stimulates abdominal organs, lungs, thyroid, rejuvenates tired legs, improves digestion, relieves menopausal symptoms, relieves menstrual pain, reduces anxiety, fatigue, back pain, headaches, insomnia. Stretches the chest, neck and the spine. Calms the brain and relieves stress and mild depression. This asana serves as a treatment for asthma, hypertension, osteoporosis, and sinusitis.

Contraindications

The one with neck Injuries has to practice with caution or, if possible, under the supervision of an experienced teacher.

3.2. Breathing techniques

(Swami Satyananda Saraswathi 2013 & Rishikul Yogashala 2013)

3.2.1. *Kapalbhati pranayama*

Kapal means "forehead/skull/brain/mind" and Bhati means "shining" in Sanskrit. Regular practice of Kapalbhati leads to a glowing face with inner radiance. Kapalbhati is a very energizing pranayama for the abdomen.

Technique

1. Be in a relaxed meditation position.

2. Close your eyes. Rest your hands on the knees and keep your palms in chin mudra or jnana mudra and relax.

3. As you exhale through both nostrils, take a deep breath inside and pull your stomach in such a way that it touches the spine. While doing this, one can sense the powerful contraction of abdominal muscles.

4. By letting the abdominal muscles relax, the inhalation should be performed passively. Without exerting any effort, the inhalation should rebound spontaneously. Continue the practice with same breathing technique for another two- three rounds of 10-20 breaths each. Should be done on an empty stomach.

Benefits

Kapalbhati has a lung purifying effect and is suitable for treating respiratory diseases. It aids in solving digestive tract problems. Strengths our mind to perform mental activities, decreases sensory disturbances and reduces drowsiness.

KAPALBHATI

Contraindications

There are certain health conditions where Kapalbhati should not be practiced especially in patients with history of cardiac disease, hypertension, epilepsy, gastric ulcers. Not recommended during pregnancy and menstruation.

3.2.2. *Sheetali pranayama (Cooling breath)*

Sheetali means coolness, calmness and peacefulness and those are the results of practicing this pranayama.

Technique

1. Assume a comfortable meditation position. Gently close your eyes and the whole body has to be relaxed.

2. Your tongue has to be extended out of your mouth. Try not to strain much while doing so. Roll the sides of the tongue in the form of a tube like a straw and inhale through your mouth if sipping air through a straw, keep your chest open and feel the cool air entering through your chest.

3. Take tongue in as you close your mouth and swallow the breath. Then gently exhale through your nose (both nostrils), empty your lungs. This is one round. Continue for 8-10 rounds per session, gradually you can increase the number of rounds.

4. Practice yogic breathing throughout. Should be done on an empty stomach.

Benefits

Sheetali Pranayama helps to reduce the body temperature that cools the body. Controls hunger and thirst and makes you feel satisfied.

Contraindications

Sheetali Pranayama should not be done in patients with history of hypotension, respiratory diseases. It is good to avoid this breathing technique during winter or in cold climates.

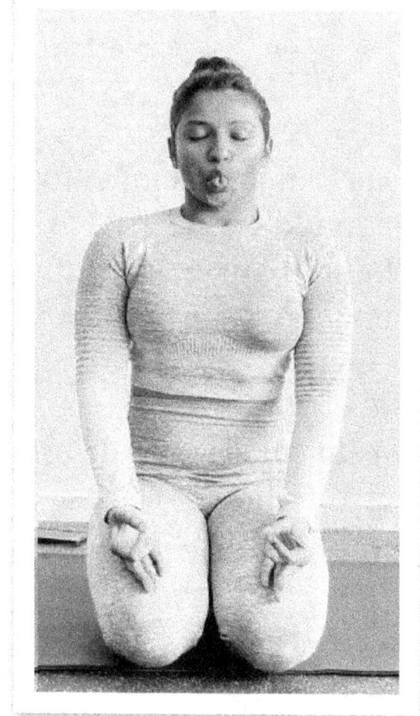

SHEETALI PRANAYAMA

3.3. Mudras

(Rishikul Yogashala 2013 & Salmon P, 2009)

3.3.1. Vayu mudra

First your index finger has to be flexed ie to be bent towards the base of your thumb and your thumb has to be placed over it as shown in the image. The other fingers should be kept extended. This reduces Vayutatva in the body.

Benefits

This is especially beneficial for those suffering from vatadosha such as arthritis, bloating of stomach etc. This increases concentration and is effective before meditation.

3.3.2. *Pushan mudra*

On your right hand, touch your thumb as shown to the tips of your right index and middle fingers. On the other hand, connect your thumb's tip to the tips of your middle and ring fingers on your left hand.

Benefits

This mudra is very helpful in managing digestive problems and diabetes. It also relieves nausea and vomiting.

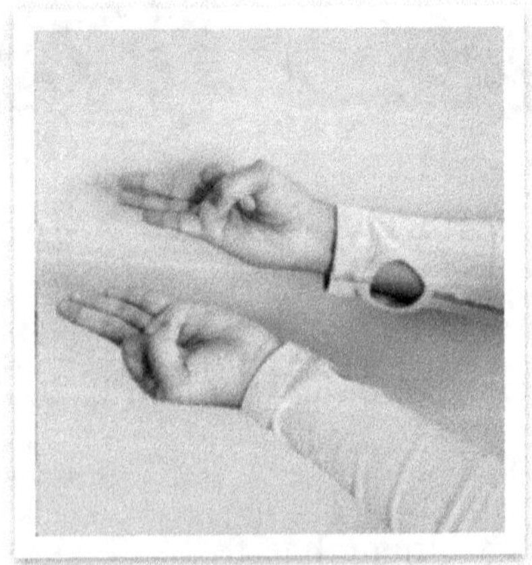

VAYU MUDRA

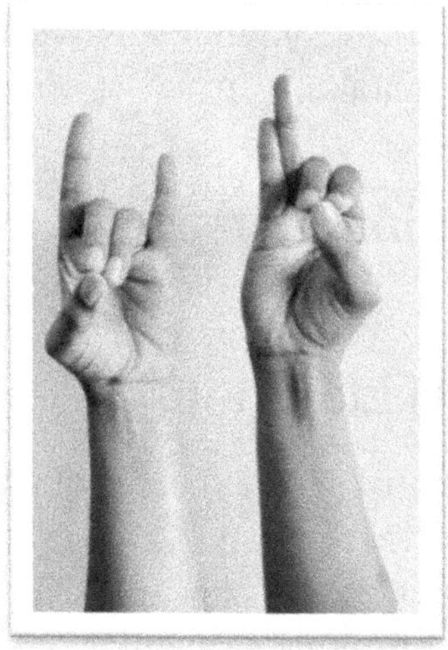

PUSHAN MUDRA

4. Conclusions

Yoga is one of the most popular mind-body exercises necessary for a person's overall health. It combines physical poses, controlled breathing, and meditation. The technique of practicing yoga improves the immune system's efficiency and reduces inflammation, which has a positive impact on mental health by lowering anxiety and depression (Salmon P et al, 2009 & Villalba Daniella K et al 2019). Even as a non-pharmacological treatment form, yoga-based interventions may be considered in IBD as a complementary option to improve patients' quality of life.

5. Acknowledgements

Authors would like to thank the Head of the Institutions of Haveri Institute of Medical Sciences, Haveri, Karnataka, India; CCR, Maldives and Shridevi

Institute of Medical Sciences & Research Hospital, Tumakuru, Karnataka, India for their support rendered.

6. Conflict of interest

None declared.

7. Ethical considerations

The photographs of Yoga Techniques in the chapter belongs to Ms. Geethanjali R, Yoga Trainer and one among the authors of this chapter & has been published after obtaining voluntary consent.

References

1. Gracie DJ, Hamlin PJ, Ford AC. The influence of the brain-gut axis in infammatory bowel disease and possible implications for treatment. Lancet Gastroenterol Hepatol. 2019;4(8):632–642. doi:10.1016/S2468-1253(19)30089-5.

2. Ng SC, Shi HY, Hamidi N, et al. Worldwide incidence and prevalence of infammatory bowel disease in the 21st century: a systematic review of population-based studies. Lancet. 2017;390(10114):2769–2778. doi:10.1016/S0140- 6736(17)32448-0.

3. Wilke E, Reindl W, Thomann PA, Ebert MP, Wuestenberg T, Thomann AK. Effects of yoga in inflammatory bowel diseases and on frequent IBD-associated extraintestinal symptoms like fatigue and depression. Complement Ther Clin

Pract. 2021 Nov;45:101465. doi: 10.1016/j.ctcp.2021.101465. Epub 2021 Jul 29. PMID: 34388560.

4. Mikocka-Walus A, Pittet V, Rossel JB, et al. Symptoms of depression and anxiety are independently associated with clinical recurrence of infammatory bowel disease. Clin Gastroenterol Hepatol. 2016;14(6):829–835.e1. doi:10.1016/j.cgh.2015.12.045

5. Anderson A, Click B, Ramos-Rivers C, et al. The association between sustained poor quality of life and future opioid use in infammatory bowel disease. Infamm Bowel Dis. 2018;24(7):1380–1388. doi:10.1093/ibd/izy040

6. Marinelli C, Savarino E, Inferrera M, et al. Factors infuencing disability and quality of life during treatment: a cross-sectional study on IBD patients. Gastroenterol Res Pract. 2019;2019:5354320.

7. Sandeep Kaur, Adrijana D'Silva, Abdel-Aziz Shaheen, Maitreyi Raman. Yoga in Patients With Infammatory Bowel Disease: A Narrative Review. Crohn's & Colitis 360. 2022;4:1–8.

8. Bernstein CN. Addressing mental health in persons with IBD. J Can Assoc Gastroenterol. 2018;1(3):97–98. doi:10.1093/jcag/gwy038.

9. Edman JS, Greeson JM, Roberts RS, et al. Perceived stress in patients with common gastrointestinal disorders: associations with

quality of life, symptoms and disease management. Explore (NY). 2017;13(2):124–128. doi:10.1016/j.explore.2016.12.005.

10. Mindful Yoga for IBD (Inflammatory Bowel Disease): Restorative Yoga Poses for IBD (Inflammatory Bowel Disease) | Tummee.com

11. Tatjana Ewais, Jake Begun, Maura Kenny, Kirsty Rickett, Karen Hay, Bita Ajilchi, Steve Kisely. A systematic review and meta-analysis of mindfulness based interventions and yoga in inflammatory bowel disease. Journal of Psychosomatic Research 2019;116:44-53.

12. Cramer, H., Schäfer, M., Schöls, M., Köcke, J., Elsenbruch, S., Lauche, R., Engler, H., Dobos, G. and Langhorst, J. Randomised clinical trial: yoga vs written self-care advice for ulcerative colitis. Aliment Pharmacol Ther.2017; 45: 1379-1389. https://doi.org/10.1111/apt.14062

13. Sharma P, Poojary G, Dwivedi SN, et al. Effect of yoga-based intervention in patients with infammatory bowel disease. Int J Yoga Therap. 2015;25(1):101–112. doi:10.17761/1531-2054-25.1.101

14. Kaur S, D'Silva A, Rajagopalan V, et al. Evaluation of an integrated yoga program in patients with infammatory bowel disease: a pilot study. EXPLORE (NY). 2022;18(3):335–341. doi:10.1016/j.explore.2021.04.006.

15. Van Aalst J, Ceccarini J, Demyttenaere K, et al. What has neuroimaging taught us on the neurobiology of yoga? A review. Front Integr Neurosci. 2020;14:34. doi:10.3389/fnint.2020.00034

16. Naveen GH, Varambally S, Thirthalli J, et al. Serum cortisol and BDNF in patients with major depression-effect of yoga. Int Rev Psychiatry. 2016;28(3):273–278. doi:10.1080/09540261.2016.11 75419

17. Holzel BK, Carmody J, Evans KC, et al. Stress reduction correlates with structural changes in the amygdala. Soc Cogn Affect Neurosci. 2010;5(1):11–17. doi:10.1093/scan/nsp034.

18. Hernández SE, Suero J, Rubia K, et al. Monitoring the neural activity of the state of mental silence while practicing Sahaja yoga meditation. J Altern Complement Med. 2015;21(3):175–179. doi:10.1089/acm.2013.0450

19. Mishra SK, Khosa S, Singh S, ct al. Changes in functional magnetic resonance imaging with. Ayu. 2017;38(3-4):108–112. doi:10.4103/ ayu.AYU_34_17.

20. Yoga Techniques for Managing IBD: Poses, Pranayama, and Mudras - Fitsri Yoga. Available at www.fitsri.com/articles/yoga-for-inflammatory-bowel-disease, cited Dec 2023.

21. Swami Satyananda Saraswathi. Asana Pranayama Mudra bandha. 2013 Edition, Yoga publications Trust, Munger, Bihar, India

22. Rishikul Yogashala. Yoga teacher training Manual. 2013, Rishikesh.

23. Salmon P, Lush E, Jablonski M, Sephton SE. Yoga and Mindfulness: Clinical Aspects of an Ancient Mind/Body Practice. *Cognitive and Behavioral Practice.* 2009 Feb;16(1):59–72. doi: 10.1016/j.cbpra.2008.07.002.

24. Villalba Daniella K, Lindsay Emily K, Marsland Anna L, Greco Carol M, Young Shinzen, Brown Kirk Warren, Smyth Joshua M, Walsh Catherine P, Gray Katarina, Chin Brian, Creswell J David. Mindfulness training and systemic low-grade inflammation in stressed community adults: Evidence from two randomized controlledtrials. *PLoSOne.* 2019;14(7):e0219120. doi: 10.1371/journal.pone.0219120.

List of Published Books

1. Gupta K and Jain M. Vridhopayogi Vyanjan: Vridhjano ke liye Upcharatmak Pak Vidhiyan. Abhinav Prakashan. Ajmer. 2016. ISBN: 978-9384189464

This book contains more than 65 healthy food recipes developed, prepared and clinically verified by myself alone, tailored with the nutritional needs of the geriatric population.

2. Gupta K. Community Science and Sustainable Community Development. Lambart Academic Publication. Germany 2021. ISBN: 978-6204197579

This book provides excellent research data related to different aspects of community which will be helpful to strengthen the sustainability of a community in terms of health, nutrition, wellness and economy.

3. Gupta K. 75 years of Indian Independence: Food and Nutritional Achievements, Opportunities and Challenges (Volume 1). Notion Press. Chennai. 2022. ISBN: 979-8888830536

4. Gupta K. 75 years of Indian Independence: Food and Nutritional Achievements, Opportunities and Challenges (Volume 2). Notion Press. Chennai. 2022. ISBN: 979-8888837573

5. Gupta K. 75 years of Indian Independence: Food and Nutritional Achievements, Opportunities and Challenges (Volume 3). Notion Press. Chennai. 2022. ISBN: 979-8889090052

These three books provide enriched research data pertaining to various aspects of health, lifestyle, tourism, agriculture, antenatal or post natal diet, nutritional status, cognition and nutrition, etc., that will be extremely helpful to improve quality of life of the individuals ultimately making healthy and sustainable community.

6. Gupta K. Aazadi ka Amrit Mahotsav: Community Science Achievements, Opportunities and Challenges. BlueRose One Publishers. India. 2023. ISBN: 978-935704938-2

This book is particularly based on different disciplines of community science, i.e., food science and nutrition, food security, advancement in food preservation and processing, sustainable breeding and cultivation approaches in agriculture, importance of prebiotics, role of therapeutic diet, importance of nutrition for pregnant ladies and children, how cognitive development is affected by nutritional status of the children, spiritual development, skill based learning system DEASA, effect of social media on community development.

7. Gupta K. Nutrition Education: An Important Pillar of Health. Notion Press. Chennai. 2023. ISBN: 979-888959915-9

This book is particularly based on different topics of nutrition science, i.e., importance of nutrition in daily life, flavours of Bengal, flavours of Ramadan, Indian spices, celebrate a world of flavours, nutrition in bed bound patients, why nutrition is essential and importance of homemade pickles in daily diet.

8. Gupta K, Bhushan V, Pandey A. Issues with Girls. Notion Press. Chennai. 2023. ISBN: 979-889026221-9

This book is particularly based on different topics related to girls and women, i.e., change in education to bring empowerment, mental hygiene, health and diet management, rise in health problems: A wake up call, girls hygiene and nutrients, letting the girls grow naturally, nutrition for girls, optimal nutrition, good health and wellbeing,: are we there yet?, women's leadership and role model for girls, empowering girls: dare to dream, baby girl: beautiful miracles.

9. Gupta K, Tripathi KM, Meena N, Sukhwal I, Soni V. Recent Trends in Community Science. BlueRose One Publishers. India. 2023. ISBN: 978-935819026-7

This book is based on different area of community science, i.e., parenting techniques and changes in parenting over the time, association between eating out and childhood obesity, rural participation and community development, ergonomics for everyone, kitchen ergonomics, use of unconventional fibres in textile industry, sustainable techniques for dye application (textile industry), spiritual development, therapeutic nutrition, impact of dietary habits on people suffering from polycystic ovarian syndrome (PCOS), millets: heritage of India, *terminalia arjuna* herb and its impact on hypercholesterolemia's patients, black cumin seeds, development disorders of children and homoeopathic treatment, success stories of women entrepreneurs from fields of community science.

10. Gupta K, Katiyar P, Meena S, Tripathi KM,. Millets: The Miracle of Nature. Notion Press. Chennai. 2023. ISBN: 979-889066606-2

This book is particularly based on topics such as millets-the nutria-cereal, magical grains, millets- the climate resilient nutria cereals, India's treasury: millets as dietary accessory, therapeutic role of millets in daily life, nutritional impact of millets on pregnant mothers, economic aspects of millets etc,.

11. Gupta K, Cherian B, Ramalakshmi, Harjai K. Health and Wellness (A basic guide to obtain good health). Notion Press. Chennai. 2023. ISBN: 979-889067222-3

Chapters of this book entitled "Health and Wellness (A basic guide to obtain good health)" particularly based on topics such as Blood, breathing & thoughts, Meditation, yoga, silence and prayer, Mind-body connection: Using yoga to enhance maternal health, Improve your low self-esteem with blessings of yoga and meditation, Food habits, Nutrition for health, Biogreens: the immunity booster, Role of nutrition in obesity, No health without mental health, Ayurveda for holistic health care, Homoeopathic biochemic treatment, Palliative care, Functional foods in cardiovascular disease, Union government initiatives to provide affordable, accessible, and quality healthcare for all.

12. Gupta K, Gaur V, Kumari R, Mishra S, Arya L, Mukharjee G. Health for All. Notion Press. Chennai. 2023. ISBN: 979-889133024-5

The edited book volume is primarily intended to be a collection of peer reviewed and plagiarism free chapters written by research scholars, academicians, scientists, doctors and faculty members of their respective fields. Chapters of this book entitled "Health for All" particularly based on topics such as sustainable innovation strategies in public health, application of technology in healthcare, world health organization's policies on world nutrition, the invisible threat of food borne diseases, obesity in affluent societies and its effect, role of nutrition education, treatment of diseases using different medical systems, non communicable diseases through workplace wellness initiatives, immunization program and serum banking in India.

13. Gupta K, Swamy D, Jain S, Sangeeta, Rochani C, Verma R. Current Advances in Community Science. Notion Press. Chennai. 2023. ISBN: 979-8891186087-2

The edited book volume is primarily intended to be a collection of peer reviewed and plagiarism free chapters particularly based on topics such as impact and benefits of nano-fertilizers, understanding the benefits of dietary fibres on health, importance of food fortification, consumer problems and protection in India related to adulteration, black marketing, health and psychological well-being, role of millets to sustain food and nutritional security, extension education in modern era, paradigm shift in extension approaches for sustainable development, computer aided designing in textiles and apparel industry, use of microfibers, Instagram as a tool to promote micro apparels and qualitative analysis on the different areas of skill development in community science.

14. Gupta K, Katiyar P, Verma P, Pawar RV, Sangeeta. Food Safety & Security- A Basic Guide. Notion Press. Chennai. 2023. ISBN: 979-889233007-7

Chapters of this book entitled "Food safety and food security (A basic guide)" particularly based on topics such as foodborne diseases, immunity boosters, feeding the nation, when food turns foul, national and international organizations working for food safety, food spoilage, food poisoning, food preservation, food safety, food security, food safety and standard authority of India (FSSAI), natural farming, food standards, food safety risk assessment and management, role of government in ensuring food safety, role of food pickles in achieving household food security, assessing the benefits and costs of improving food safety.

15. Gupta K, Venkatappa KG, Devi KV, Sangeeta, Pal P. Brain: Associations, Wellness & Treatment. Notion Press. Chennai. 2024. ISBN: 979-8892233671-0

Chapters of this book entitled **"Brain: Associations, Wellness and Treatment"** particularly based on topics such as brain health and disabilities, what I learnt about our brain, heads off to migraine, effect of stress on mental health, unlocking mental wellness, Parkinson's disease and its homeopathic treatment, mental health, depression, interrelation between brain health and cognitive functioning, artificial intelligence and cognitive science, effect of sleep patterns on brain health, prioritizing brain health, spirituality and brain health, impact of financial condition on brain heath, drugs and brain health; and impact of homemade food on maintaining brain health and wellness.

Note: These books are available on publisher's website, Amazon and FlipKart